D0053689

WITHDRAWN
UTSA Libraries

RENEWALS 691-4574
DATE DUE

AP

[

COPYRIGHTS IN THE WORLD MARKETPLACE

Successful Approaches to International Media Rights

COPYRIGHTS
IN THE WORLD
MARKETPLACE

Successful Approaches to
International Media Rights

by Richard Wincor

 PRENTICE HALL LAW & BUSINESS

Library
University of Texas
at San Antonio

Copyright © 1990 by Richard Wincor.
All rights reserved. No part of this publication may
be reproduced or transmitted in any form or by any means,
electronic or mechanical, including photocopy, recording, or any
information storage and retrieval system, without permission in
writing from the publisher.

Requests for permission to make copies of any part of the work
should be mailed to:
Permissions, Prentice Hall Law & Business
270 Sylvan Avenue, Englewood Cliffs, NJ 07632

Printed in the United States of America

Library of Congress Cataloging in Publication Data

Wincor, Richard.
    Copyrights in the world marketplace / Richard Wincor.
      p. cm.
    Includes index
    ISBN 0-13-173956-5
    1. Copyright. 2. Copyright, International. I. Title.
    K1420.5.W55 1990
    341.7'582 – dc20   90-14293
                                                               CIP

Library
University of Texas
at San Antonio

For Molly and Daisy

TABLE OF CONTENTS

Table of Contents

INTRODUCTION

Suddenly, or so it appears, copyrights have been promoted from pawns to queens on the global chessboard. Originally the province of artistes and their patrons, then growing into major industries, copyrights and their companion trademarks now preoccupy those conducting affairs of state. Treaties and trade preferences complement national laws against piracy. Incorporeal assets worth billions leap national boundaries within seconds. Database is a new literature, the computer a co-author and the satellite an incomparable carrier. Still, even in this Age of Software, the more traditional arts flourish and in some cases allay or incite political unrest. In short, transmedia communications are a new empire, and all of us are its subjects.

Then too, there are some who serve as its administrators. These include lawyers, publishers, producers, literary agents and of course those possessed of creative talent whose writings and other brainchildren inhabit the latest hardware. For these professionals many guides are available. Nearly every country that produces or consumes intellectual property has its own literature on this arcane craft. In the main this literature consists of treatises, case books, contract forms and learned articles indispensable for the conduct of media transactions.

And yet, understandably, perhaps, something is missing in

the professional literature, namely a concise overview of key points that arise with international trade in communications. Collections of case precedents have no place here. Quite different concerns need to be addressed, issues strangely elusive and difficult of orderly presentation. The attempt is a little daunting, but worth a try. One may find relatively few answers – laws differ country to country anyway – but the key thing is asking the right questions. Only in that way can the spectacular pitfalls in this area be avoided.

This handbook, then, is addressed to those concerned with copyrights in the world marketplace. It reflects international contract patterns untied to the laws of any particular country, although American and British usages predominate. Step by step, it records a particular approach (calling it an informed approach may go too far) in dealing with those problems that bedevil the delivery of intellectual property to global markets.

Specific contract phrases appear every now and then, but only as examples. Routine clauses such as provisions for the furnishing of notice are omitted completely. My concern, instead, is with major points that often must be perceived and analyzed under intense time pressure. These are put forward on hypothetical facts reflecting the experience of actual events.

The Part One material is presented in a series of chapters. The sequence is plausible but could be varied. Although the reflections under each caption are unequal in length, they are close to equal in importance. Part Two furnishes contract examples with commentary.

Non-specialists may find the idea groupings the equivalent of a crash course in a foreign language, enough to get by under the right conditions. The specialist is another matter. One hopes that something in the discussion may prove of interest even to those familiar with the terrain. Much of it, after all, is unmapped.

The analysis is developed informally, somewhat as a dialogue with the reader, and is designed mainly to impart a conceptual vocabulary. Scenes change with unnatural speed in the communications industries. New technology requires constant pioneering. There are few neat solutions, but recognition of patterns is the key to survival.

The initiate, then, will be undismayed when a device landed on Jupiter transmits pictures with text of its own composition.

Who owns Japanese language rights? Was the work done for hire, and under whose law? Can the rights claimant give proper warranties? Do the contracts collide with treaties?

Answers may be elusive, but at least you will be asking the right questions.

Richard Wincor
New York City 1990

Part I

Part I

Chapter 1

PRELIMINARY CONSIDERATIONS

The first thing to be said about works of authorship is that by nature they elude confinement to a fixed locale. At the moment of creation they become international, floating, or having the capacity to do so, across national borders, across oceans, and potentially from one medium to another as the world's most cosmopolitan product. Being incorporeal, they are unbounded by walls and fences. Only the law defines their boundaries, and contracts mark out their measurements.

It follows that media rights cannot be analyzed solely in local terms. Questions such as "Is this material still in copyright?" or "Who owns X's version of Y?" may be off the mark. They cannot really be answered without asking, "Where?" And as if this were not enough, you may also need to be concerned with "When" particular events occurred since authorship in a certain era may have produced one lasting result while the same activity under a reformed copyright regime may have led to a different outcome in the same country. A closer look is required.

Locale

Locale comes first. More specific questions concerning time and place will be explored in a later section on copyright, but in

3

this earliest phase we glance at the entire canvas. Let us assume, for example, that a television production company sells its filmed dramatization of a British novel to a U.S. network. The producer has gone to the trouble of confirming that the novel is in the public domain. Accordingly, it would appear that no permission is needed for the adaptation and, further, that no royalties will be going to the author's estate in England. Only the script writer will be paid. On this easy assumption, the producer agrees that the network is to have its "usual coverage" for the U.S. and Canada. A contract to that effect is prepared.

The position, however, may be not as simple as it appears. Conceivably, and depending in part on when it all happens, the novel is still protected by copyright in England, and rather more to the point, in Canada. Therefore performance in Canada constitutes an infringement. Even if Canadian rights are withdrawn for that reason, one can imagine a signal crossing the border from Michigan to Ontario. Then new concerns arise; Mexico is next door to California, so that a signal from San Diego may cross into a station in Tijuana. Television signals may form the advance units of unintended infringement because nobody thought internationally. Difficulties of this kind are unlikely, but they are plausible.

Why should it be of concern except to litigators? Because awareness of such pitfalls can be reflected in contracts. Perhaps the territory will be confined, or responsibilities for the risk divided by advance agreement. Perhaps the obstructing rights will be cleared by a contract to pay the British rights owner's estate. Solutions vary; the thing is to develop a sixth sense for these potential problems.

Time and Legal Regime

Time as well as space comes into this first overview. Time, in this case, means the copyright regime in effect when key incidents occurred. Here too, as with geographic locale, one should see the invisible and hear the inaudible. Another Anglo-American example illustrates the point.

Suppose an American publisher brings out a distinguished

series of works by a deceased British author pursuant to the author's contract with a London publisher who could, and in fact did, lay off U.S. rights on the Americans. The British have given the Americans their publishing rights "for the full term of copyright." Nobody sees clouds on the horizon. In the distance, however, they may be gathering.

There used to be a section in the UK Copyright Act effecting reversion of rights to an author's estate twenty-five years *post mortem*. The philosophy behind this provision, which has been abolished, was to protect the families of authors from that unworldliness with which the creative genius is too often afflicted. Its effect on publishers, however, can readily be imagined. One minute they had the rights, the next minute they didn't. Not many licensees knew the risks involved.

Now for the dilemma: twenty-five years slip away and the author's estate recaptures his rights from the British publisher. With an eye toward negotiating better royalties, the heirs notify the American publishers that their rights have expired along with their British source. "What!" say the Americans, "This British reversion law has no force in the United States." The heirs see it differently: their British publisher never could have granted the Americans greater rights than it possessed on its own, and twenty-five years was all it ever had. When that period expired, the rest fell like dominos, and therefore, by sheer logic, the Americans are out.

Which side wins? Suggesting an answer to that question is not really our concern here. The larger issue is whether anything in this recital has contract implications. It does; you need only consider somebody negotiating a sublicense from the American publisher. That sublicense may fall with its American support if the domino theory stands up for the British heirs. How the proposed sublicensee anticipates this in contract is a separate matter. There could be warranties that no reversion will occur, or perhaps repayment coupled with first refusal on alternative rights. Many solutions are possible; the point is to be aware that foreign laws from a past era may still obstruct business arrangements. The past era side of it is our focus here. England's twenty-five year reversion law was repealed years ago, but not retroactively. Fossils of this kind still can trip the unwary.

Accordingly, time as well as space, the era when laws were different from those currently in effect, should be part of any first analysis.

An easier case, putting aside international dimensions in this instance, is the "C" in a circle copyright notice on published material. Its omission was fatal in the United States before 1978 if the copyright owner allowed it. After 1978, its omission was serious but curable, due to new legislation. Starting in 1989, however, it could be left off, except that infringers could then claim innocence through failure to be put on notice. In short, the formality of notice is linked to successive copyright regimes. First impressions of a published work inspire not only the question where, but when its earlier history developed.

The underlying point of these examples concerns the inadequacy of easy conclusions that This is in copyright, and That isn't. In copyright *where?* If Singapore is a proposed market, what was the law there on the date of UK publication? What about Germany? These are the questions that arise with all but domestic markets. We consider them not to guide litigation, but to prevent it. That is our mission here, and good contracts are the machinery for its accomplishment.

Market Potential

Another element deserves mention before we take up international media contracts in more detail, namely market potential. Rarely will you have everything your own way. It helps, accordingly, to have priorities in mind for the campaigns ahead. These priorities will vary according to the material under negotiation — writings are not sausages — and therefore some rights can be scuttled with one work, but not with another. Here are some examples:

With a novel, author and publisher will contest film and television rights;

With scientific or other technical material, rights in the database loom larger;

Children's books frequently engender merchandising, with products based on fictional characters.

And so it goes; certainly these evaluations can turn out wrong, but they are worth attempting. Whatever product is entered for negotiation deserves better than indifference to its unique potentials. Works of authorship react poorly to uniform treatment.

Chapter 2
COPYRIGHT

How do you copyright something? This frequently posed question reflects assumptions that are at least partly wrong. Whoever raises it probably has registration in mind, filling out forms for deposit in some central registry and thereby creating something out of nothing. The resultant something is "a copyright" and this, in turn, is sometimes equated with distribution rights, or publication rights, or a certificate bearing an official's signature.

This is not, however, what really happens. Neither is a popular version of what happens next, that the new-born copyright, armed with certificates and receipts for deposit fees, protects the owner against poachers of all sorts except those who borrow some fixed number of lines and bars, or images, without permission. Collectively these beliefs constitute a mythology all their own. Our mission is to dispel the myths and replace them with a practical outline of fundamentals.

Securing Copyright

To begin with, copyright is secured by the mere act of creation. Formalities such as imprinting "C" in a circle and depositing copies have their place (one that shrinks roughly decade by decade), but these steps are not essential for securing copyright. Creation does it, and now we hedge a little, with three caveats.

For one thing, the author needs evidence to prove authorship. That should scarcely be a problem even if recording in the Copyright Office before publication is dispensed with.

Second, it must be remembered that mere ideas, systems, slogans and even titles are not protected by copyright. Only their specific form of expression is encompassed by the protective wall, not the rules of a game, for example, but their exposition by pamphlet, and its diagrams. Some minimal substance is essential, more than mere trivia.

Third the material for which copyright is sought must be written down, or fixed in some other tangible form (although requirements vary from country to country). Oral composition on its own will not always suffice.

Subject to these modest qualifications, creation creates copyright. This, at least, is the general approach in most countries.

Benefits of Copyright

What happens next? What have you got as a result of securing copyright? Here are some chief benefits:

a) In most national legislation, protection for a term measured by the author's life plus fifty years (the Germans enacted life plus seventy);

b) Exclusive rights not only to prevent copying, but to make adaptations for other media, translations and other versions of the original material known as "derivative works";

c) Exclusive rights to reproduce, perform publicly and otherwise turn to account certain material;

d) Where treaties and conventions are in place, protection abroad; and

e) In some countries, a right known as the *droit moral*, or "moral right," to claim paternity of one's work through authorship credit, and to prevent distortion of the material.

Points Often Overlooked

Again, even with a minimalist approach, a bit of embellishment is necessary. Exclusive rights, for example, are exclusive only up to a point. In certain circumstances outsiders are allowed what the Americans call Fair Use, and the British call Fair Dealing, with limited segments of protected material for scholarly or other purposes. Then too, with recorded music, a compulsory license for royalties fixed by statute may be available for outsiders. In other words, copyright is something less than a complete monopoly.

A more remarkable observation is that some of the most valuable components of literary property exist in a legal limbo, their status and credentials undefined. Most famous among these is the fictional character extracted from its engendering work and spun off into new and highly lucrative adventures. What is Sherlock Holmes? Can verbal portraits without graphics create property? Must the rights in characters die out when the copyright in their birthplace story expires? These and other mysteries are still unsolved.

The compendium of facts dilemma also eludes solution. Should the database be protected, and does hard work or originality in the compilation attract greater protection? Here, too, the law is unsettled at a time when computers are boosting assemblages of facts into a new literature. Copyright borders are not always distinct.

Differences in National Treatment

Our sampling of main principles distilled laws from a number of countries that respect copyright. Up to a point, that outlines the ground rules, but then national differences intrude. Holland, for example, recognizes works made for hire as belonging to the employer. So does the United States, of course with different standards, but German copyright law goes the opposite way. There is no such thing in the German system.

Does it make a difference for professionals concerned chiefly with contract? It does, even if you are not hiring Dutch or German writers for a project on petroleum reserves. The international framework is where events in the communications industries unfold. World markets are their natural setting, and so there is no way to divide them by contract without awareness, if not mastery, of treaty law.

Most countries that export and import literature are linked by copyright treaties. Many of these began as bilateral arrangements in the 19th century. In time they were replaced, or in some cases supplemented, with multilateral conventions among industrialized nations. Today all sorts of special arrangements exist dealing with everything from satellite broadcasts to phonograms. The two most important copyright treaties are the Universal Copyright Convention and the Berne Convention, together with its successive amendments. Perhaps too, one should mention the European Community even though it is scarcely a copyright edifice. Its unpredictability, especially as a challenge to the exclusivity of rights traditionally carved out in media contracts, requires that it be kept under constant watch.

A multilateral copyright union aims at national treatment, equalizing the protection given authors of works originating in the union framework on one hand, and protection for one's own nationals on the other. Berne can actually result in better terms for foreigners. For example, exemptions are provided from certain formalities. Nevertheless, some of the signatory countries follow the rule of the shorter term whereby protection for foreigners endures for whichever is shorter as between the law of the protecting country and the country of origin.

Moreover, the conventions are not necessarily self-executing. The United States, for example, required implementing legislation to amend its Copyright Act when it joined Berne. Thus you cannot go into an American court brandishing the Berne Convention as such, but only its reflection in domestic statute, and this of course allows disparities between levels of protection one country to another. British tradition is unreceptive to the self-executing approach and in some countries one must consider legislation as possibly superseding a Convention text. Then too, the various treaties and conventions stop short of resolving conflicts of law problems or disputes essentially about contract interpretation.*

That these multinational points are not irrelevant to contract dealings becomes evident at a glance. Consider, for example, the American copyright renewal required for a second copyright term; this is phased out now, except for works in their original twenty-eight year term on January 1, 1978. But anyone planning to buy writings whose owner forgot to effect timely renewal will want to find out how this omission affects copyright outside the United States. The material may still be protected in Australia, or then again, perhaps not. An Australian legal opinion may be required.

As further example, a Swiss company may plan opening a subsidiary outside Switzerland for the publication of a financial newsletter. One of various considerations besides tax will be copyright. Shall it be Holland or France? Will the place of production have more than marginal effect? The managing director worries about *droit moral* even with staff writers; without company ability to change written material at the last minute, publication will be at major risk. Does the country of choice enforce *droit moral?* Can it be waived as an "adaptation," and complete ownership vested in the employer? As a practical matter, do writers contract it away for good salaries? Here too, local opinions of law may guide the decision. One must keep current, especially when foreign contract waivers come before courts in France, or Italy, or elsewhere.

Commissioning an informed opinion requires asking the right questions. These will never occur to somebody who is unaware of the complexities with world markets. We are not still the Roman empire, and not yet a gigantic Benelux. Treaties or no treaties, copyright has its national borders. In crossing some, you may even encounter laws that impede licensing.

---

*These problems are too complex for any sort of casual treatment. Anyone interested in exploring them further will do well to consult Professor Ulmer's study entitled *Intellectual Property Rights and the Conflict of Laws* (The Netherlands 1978) and Paul Geller's Introduction to Nimmer and Geller, *International Copyright Law and Practice* (New York 1989).

Awareness of this framework is useful, but copyright is not the sole stuff of which the property in communications is made. There is a companion doctrine, less famous in the media, which sometimes picks up where copyright leaves off, and is too frequently ignored even in sophisticated contracts. That doctrine is trademark law.

Chapter 3

TRADEMARK

An important development in the law of intellectual property is the growing usefulness of trademarks as adjuncts to copyrights. Copyrights fall short of protecting titles and logo emblems, as well as serial uses such as *Encyclopedia Britannica* where repetition rather than originality is a chief ingredient for protection. In this respect trademark law may be able to accomplish what copyright cannot, investing the symbolic badges with a different sort of protection governed by different rules. The significance of its potential as a rescue device is too little appreciated. Theoretically at least, and with glimmerings of support in the authorities, trademark elements in works of literature may survive the expiration of copyright, continuing to protect just enough of the material they symbolize to keep poachers away. Naturally the argument against this approach is that the owner is coming round the back door when lawfully denied entry via the front. In other words, it seems an attempt to extend copyright beyond its permitted term.

Nevertheless, trademarks are worth looking for in the analysis of writings and other communications. So are their counterparts known as service marks, symbols for services rather than products, although the distinction is not always clear. Harrods, for example, make Christmas puddings; on these articles the name would serve as a trademark. If a department of that institution delivered the puddings beyond Knightsbridge, its name could be functioning as a service mark; and behind all of it, standing in dowdy grandeur, is the institution itself where the key word serves as a trade name. For convenience, however, we set aside these distinctions and refer to the entire lot as trademarks. In what follows, we consider briefly how a body of law usually identified with cars and cereals turns up in the intangible empires of recorded communications.

How Secured; Scope of Protection

The law itself, as earlier mentioned, is quite different from copyright. Use, or occasionally the intent to use, is what creates rights in the United States. Registration is also important, despite the availability of common law protection in some instances. Moreover, trademark registration procedures are more expensive, time-consuming and complex than those pertaining to copyright. The ambit of protection, however, is circumscribed, as with copyright. An American trademark, for example, is unlikely to afford its owner a complete monopoly for the name as against all other products and services. The idea is to shield consumers from the likelihood of confusion on encountering familiar brand names. Corporate diversification through mergers and acquisitions has enlarged many zones of potential business expansion, but there are still limits. Nobody is likely to assume that Rolls-Royce shoes come from the famous motor company.

And yet, as so often happens, there is a notable exception in trademark law. Many of the American states have enacted statutes creating rights and remedies against "dilution." These anti-dilution laws forbid use of another's name – usually a famous name, as it works out – on completely disparate products that no reasonable consumer would buy as emanating from the original source. The dilution theory, Germanic in background, protects against whittling away the magic sales power of a trademark by rival use even in unrelated fields. This doctrine is by no means universally accepted, and of course trademark laws differ from country to country without anything as wide-ranging as Berne in copyright, although regional treaties are currently in place.

Trademarks, like copyrights, are licensed by contract but the rules are different. American law, for example, requires that the licensor maintain "quality control" over the licensed products so as to avoid confusing the public into buying B's product thinking it was A's because of the name. Inspecting samples and other control measures may in some circumstances be accomplished by deputies, but the control must be there and should be recited in contract. Publishing and other industries have not yet taken enough advantage of reciting trademark ownership and control in their agreements when trademarks are in fact established in series titles, certain characters and other material. They may be missing out on a new level of protection by contract.

Conceptually different from trademark licensing is the Consent to Use device. Here, usually after a dispute, neither side recognizes ownership by the other in the disputed area. Instead of a license between owner and user you have a form of peace treaty dividing use of the disputed mark by spheres. This approach, more familiar in copyright management, requires no quality control because nobody is affirmatively granting rights to anyone else. The contracting parties are just drawing lines, marking out turf. Consent to Use contracts often are full of pious assurances, present for easily confused customers, that no marketplace confusion will occur even if two companies use the same mark.

Fictional Characters

There exists, however, one commodity so unique, so unsettled in legal status, and yet so astonishingly income-producing that it requires separate discussion. This commodity (calling it so seems heresy) is the fictional character. Nowadays character licensing is major industry. Extracted from books and set to new adventures in television and merchandising, characters can earn millions for their owners. Sometimes the process goes roundabout, television to books and then back again; the transmedia potentials are endless. In merchandising especially, the character brings harvest. Then it becomes toys, or clothing, or edibles, even theme parks until it inhabits books again with enriched material from other media.

But what is a character of fiction? Not a copyright in itself, although often protected as part of a novel. Plucked out of its old setting, however, it lives on its own. Transplanted, it earns its own way. Ultimately, the story engendering it falls into the public domain. Does its hero survive the vehicle? Perhaps so, if this component of copyright has in fact grown into a trademark. Whether or not this has happened varies from case to case. It happens infrequently, but the potential is there.

Visual characters are the best bet. Names and cartoons inch toward trademark status, but surely characters are something beyond outward appearance. Verbal portraits are what capture their true essence. Let us consider a few examples as trademark candidates. Their admission to that status may be worth fortunes.

Stereotypes neither attract nor deserve any protection at all. A step toward something more distinctive, however, is the character made vivid through reference by others, but who never (or belatedly) appears. In that category you find Daphne du Maurier's *Rebecca*, and a woman called Mavis from early Australian television. Now add another element, but still hearsay, a sobriquet such as "Himmler of the lower fifth" used about the unpopular schoolmaster Crocker-Harris in Terence Rattigan's play *The Browning Version*. This repeated phrase sounds a little like a trademark in the process of formation. Still, however, it remains what others are saying, not the character himself.

A phrase repeated by the character himself brings us a step further. In Farquhar's *The Beaux' Strategem* we find this fragment in Act 1 Scene 1:

"Aimwell
'You're my landlord, I suppose?'
"Boniface
'Yes Sir, I'm old Will Boniface, pretty well known, upon the
     road, as the saying is' . . .
"Aimwell
'O Mr. Boniface, your servant.' "
"Boniface
'O Sir, what will your Honor please to drink, as the saying
     is?' "

Pretty thin stuff (as the saying is), but catchy. A more famous example is "Bah, humbug" but here the phrase is part of something richer, and paradoxically, for that very reason, less promising as a trademark. Scrooge is Frazer's dying and resurrected god-king from *The Golden Bough*. This is what makes him immortal, not his conversion to good works at Christmas. If Dickens were still in copyright, Scrooge as a licensing asset might prove marginal.

Perhaps the ultimate step is a style of speaking that identifies the speaker. Claude Mauriac's novel *The Dinner Party* presents speakers without name attribution, but we can tell nevertheless who is speaking. A trademark style appears in the following extract from Sheridan's *The Rivals*, Act III scene iii, but here we have a character name that has itself become generic:

"There, sir, an attack upon my language! What do you think of that?—an aspersion upon my parts of speech! Was ever such a brute! Sure, if I reprehend any thing in this world be it the use of my oracular tongue, and a nice derangement of epitaphs!"

Thus speaks Mrs. Malaprop. Even more vivid is Mr. Jingle from *Pickwick:*

" 'Heads, heads—take care of your heads!' cried the loquacious stranger, as they came out under the low archway, which in those days formed the entrance to the coach-yard. 'Terrible place—dangerous work—other day—five children—mother-tall lady, eating sandwiches—forgot the arch—crash—knock—children look round—mother's head off—sandwich in her hand—no mouth to put it in—head of a family off—shocking, shocking! Looking at Whitehall, sir?—fine place—little window—somebody else's head off there, eh, sir? he didn't keep a sharp look-out enough either—eh, sir, eh?' "

Jingle brings instant recognition. Whether his style rather than trademark phrases could be protected nowadays is unclear. Questions of that sort will remain unsettled until we accept characters for what they are, a new form of property.

Meanwhile we have trademarks to supplement copyright.

Even fictitious locales may acquire the "secondary meaning" that supports some of the less distinctive marks which still attract certain levels of protection. Narnia, Brigadoon, Ruritania—but the point has been made. Fictitious devices have lives of their own.

Some of them, not only titles, can be laid claim to in contracts. Call a trademark a trademark, even if it still is in the process of becoming one. That way, at least, you can spell out who owns it.

Chapter 4

A SAMPLE MISSION

Armed at least with enough background for spotting issues, one comes now to the application of theory in real contracts. Everything next is "practical"; and consistent with this approach, we glance first at how international rights transactions are likely to begin. Later on we follow them through, point by point, but they are unlikely to arise out of a vacuum. Rights acquisitions grow out of real business ventures that have beginnings and endings. And so we now consider a multinational acquisition in its earliest state.

In this exercise an American company acquires television rights to a British novel which incorporates German material. That sounds straightforward enough, but it reflects nothing of the literary detective work required for accomplishment of the mission. Here are the main hypothetical players:

a) An American publishing house with an eye on audiovisual markets;
b) Their lawyers;
c) The British novelist's estate;
d) Its publisher;
e) Its literary agent;

g) Its lawyer; and

h) The German author of material quoted in the book.

Those listed as (a) and (b) are collectively referred to as "the Licensees" and the others are grouped as "the Owners" although in the latter instance their status is currently not proved.

How should the acquisition begin? A first point is to get the instructions straight. A lawyer assigned to securing "television rights" will be aware that the phrase has no fixed meaning. Does it include cable? Must Japanese rights be part of it? Videocassette, novelization, all that? But we run ahead of the mission; enough at this stage to say that instructions in this field are often vague, reflecting at times a certain modesty of comprehension in the person giving them. Assume for convenience that the instructions are simply to do one's best. That way we get more quickly into the right procedures.

First Steps

There are three things to be done at the outset. Their sequence varies according to circumstance and convenience, but in effect they happen all at the same time. All three are measures undertaken by the Licensees as the side initiating this transaction. Here is what you do as their representative:

First, order a copyright search from a professional service. It starts you off—probably nothing more—on the great treasure hunt for the rights, and besides that it will look unprofessional if your financiers or successors in interest ask for it and learn that nothing was ever done.

Second, ring up the publishers and ask who controls television rights to the Property. Their "Rights and Permissions" administrator will look it up for you in their contract with the author. Nowadays odds are she will tell you the author controls television rights even though the publishers may be entitled to a share of proceeds from their disposition. Accordingly, she will refer you to the author's agent, now agent for her estate.

A third step, however, is the most challenging and may prove the most rewarding of all among these initial measures. It requires looking at the Property itself. What, you must be thinking, must I plod through five hundred pages of rubbish? Of course not, but half an hour's browse may be invaluable. It was suggested earlier that examining the product guides you in evaluating which rights are the more important.

Copyright Notice and Beyond

Then too there is the "C" in a circle copyright notice. This emblem is only a beginning. Its omission may or may not thrust the work into the public domain depending, as earlier noted, on when it was published. Omission in any event is no reason to assume public domain status outside the United States if foreign markets are of interest. For that matter, finding that something is in the public domain is not always a reason for rejoicing. It means there is no way to acquire exclusivity, and that rivals may produce the same work sooner and better. Even the prospect of such intrusion may make it impossible to secure financing.

In most cases, there will be a copyright notice. This, however, is only a beginning. The named owner may in fact be holding copyright in trust for somebody else. More likely still, the copyright is encumbered with various license agreements that no search of official registries will fully disclose. Assignments may turn up, but not all of the grants of film rights or first refusals on merchandising. One must talk to the other side.

The book, let us say, is the story of a Colonel's widow destroyed by inflation. Somewhere in the middle it incorporates an extended segment of a history of inflation from Roman times to Weimar by a professor from Berlin. We ask whether the rights to this German material were cleared. We are assured that they were. We look doubtful. The other side offers to show us the documentation. It consists of an old telegram from the British publisher to be the German publisher saying

"Dear Sirs:

We are publishing a novel by Chastity Lightfoot entitled *Twelve Per Cent Annually* and find that she has incorporated most of

Chapter Three from your *History of Inflation* by Otto Kleinkopf.
May we use it?"

And the reply says "Ja."

Now this is exactly the sort of thing that goes on far too
often, confusing everybody. "Ja" to what, one UK hardcover? An
American paperback? Films, television, computer software? The
inflation database is summed up and published separately in a
business manual. Are these uses covered by the original permission or is nearly every one of them an infringement? Does (or did)
German law treat disputes arising from these ambiguities as
copyright or contract matters? Does the publisher have sufficient
rights from Kleinkopf?

Besides all that there is another catch. Someone, it will occur
to us, must have translated the German material into English.
Who cleared the translator's rights in the English derivative? If
anyone did, was the permission less ambiguous that with
Kleinkopf's German? Was the translation done as work made for
hire, if that arrangement was lawful at the time? And lawful
under English or German law? If the German author or publisher
had the rights, were they assignable? Would the language have
covered television? Did the British reversion right come into it
somewhere? Did the translator contract preclude the making of
other translations through a mandatory "merger" clause?

So much for casual arrangements. They can land you in
tangles of epic proportion. On the other hand, serious attention to
these matters at the outset is a sound investment.

This imaginary launch of a rights acquisition has no ending.
Perhaps the entire clearance process will be done over from the
beginning, consuming a year to work out royalties. Perhaps the
Licensees will proceed without further documentation, eventually losing in court. The production funding might be withdrawn,
once the chain of title appeared fragile. Or, perhaps, nothing will
go wrong at all. Surely, though, the odds are unacceptable.
Timely analysis is required to save the day.

Chapter 5

THE GRANT OF RIGHTS

With media contracts a key provision, often central to a constellation of points, is the grant of rights. By this is meant the recital, frequently at some length, of how the rights owner permits the licensee to use the owner's material. Usually the term, the territories, the media and the degree of exclusivity are spelled out but grant provisions differ widely as they reflect different business arrangements. The common denominator, however, is an authorization to use, and perhaps allow others to use, literary or other property in a certain way. Sometimes additional uses are available on option or if certain conditions are met. Those rights that are not granted are reserved for the owner but may be encumbered, restricted or subjected to any number of conditions, all of them made clear in a reservation of rights clause and its companion provisions. These various hedges, however, are not what is meant here by the grant of rights. They are ancillary to it, just as payment for the rights is of major importance but stands separately. A grant of rights sets out the boundaries of agreed usage.

By way of aside, or perhaps of reinforcement, the concept of exclusivity is crucial here. Informal deal memoranda drawn up even in high places often omit the key word, possibly in the heat of engagement or because its presence by implication is assumed.

That assumption is dangerous. Compressed phrases such as "the exclusive, transferable right but not obligation" are good shorthand phrases for grantees under time pressure.

Adversarial Nature of Owner-Grantee Relationship

The relationship between rights owner and grantee is essentially adversarial. At this stage we can defer discussion of computer-assisted creation and other collaborations and deal instead with the classic duo: author and publisher. Typically the author reserves whatever can be held back from the publisher, while the publisher seeks to control all rights in the author's work forever. Since their bargaining positions are usually unequal, the author's reservation of key rights may not be possible.

Sometimes, when the grantee or user has special competence in a particular area, it may suit the rights owner to include that in the grant, at least for a trial period subject to reversion for non-performance. Special competence may be an audiovisual department with major credits, or a branch office in Tokyo. The owner's agent may resist any enlargement of the grant, often with good reason, but that raises another issue.

Literary Agents

Literary agents acting as such are participants in proceeds but are not rights transferees. Usually they "own" nothing except rights to commission certain transactions. For this reason, any long discussion of agency arrangements would be out of place here. Nevertheless some brief reflections may be of use.

An obvious question is what a ten or fifteen percent commission (larger in merchandising) is founded on. Should the agent have exclusivity and be paid for transactions accomplished by somebody else? Does agency representation mean participation in all countries, all media, all versions? And what if a rights owner turns producer and receives millions in financing which are paid out for budget elements, can the agent commission the gross? Surely not, in the last example, but agency arrangements are not always in writing. That they ought to be is clear even from these few examples.

If further demonstration is needed, it can be found at the foot of many publishing contracts where a clause making the author's agent a sort of third party beneficiary entitled to percentages of royalties under the publishing agreement (that dangerous word, "hereunder") constitutes the only documentation covering agency commissions. What if film rights are sold, but not by the agent? "Hereunder" may loom large; if the publisher got the film rights under a different clause, then the agent might contend that the film sale was in fact something accomplished under the contract and therefore commissionable. However, if the author held the film rights back from the publisher, then the agent's claim for commissions would seem weaker. If film rights had for some reason been held back and later included by amendment, a classic muddle on agency commissions could result. All of this could have been avoided by a sensible agency agreement.

Defining the Property with Precision

All too often the contracting parties fail to spell out precisely what material is to be the subject of the rights transfer. A complete entity such as a code book will be called "the Work" or a drama "the Play," but we are not told which version of the code book is meant, or whether the play includes its Dutch translation with incidental music. With something less than complete entities, fictional characters for example, vagueness of description is even more prevalent. Would rights to Scrooge have encompassed his reformed persona, now keen on Christmas? Clearly the same extremist perhaps, but what of a cartoon character whose name or depiction changes? What about a performer who plays herself or a character she has made her own? Merely reciting the name, and then referring to it as "the Property," may not be good enough. What the Property consists of should be pinned down. Occasionally there may be good reason for having it vague, but more often than not this will lead to trouble. Evasive or overly casual descriptions can be avoided with only a little difficulty in most instances. Land grants are measured carefully, and literary grants deserve equal care. In sum, definition of the "Property" is an essential exercise.

Something which is a license of incorporeals appears all too often as a catalogue of hardware. Worse, the hardware is antiquated by new technology long before the license expires. Early American television contracts sound out of date now, with "3-D," "CATV" and other acrostics reflecting the latest things in communications, one referring to dimension and the other to community antenna. Today more advanced modes of delivering signals are recited in contract clauses, but we can never keep up. Technology outmodes even the best boilerplate and the rule of *inclusio unus exclusio alterius* lurks in the background reminding us that whatever we fail to include in our list may be deemed purposely excluded for that reason.

This is not to say, however, that specific media never should be mentioned. The point, rather, is that great care is required when you are doing it. If it seems necessary to mention a specific cable facility in addition to "all existing and future audiovisual devices" or something to that effect, "including without limitation" is essential wording as prelude.

That the term, territory and medium encompassed in a grant are key points is self-evident, but whether licensee failure to meet performance standards in one area should forfeit everything is a harder question. So, too, is exclusivity.

Exclusivity

A vital concept in nearly every rights negotiation is exclusivity. This element, sometimes given completely but more often restricted to specified areas, has a major impact on everything from price to whether or not any sale occurs at all. Investing money and time in the development of properties that are also available to competitors is nobody's first choice, but the licensee rarely gets everything. That would be an outright assignment of copyright, which is not usually what happens. Instead there is a series of exclusive grants, rights partitioned among several users, each likely to possess some measure of exclusivity. Sometimes this may be complete, if only in a given language and territory, such as the exclusive right to publish an English-language hardcover book in the United States and Canada. Other territories, however, may be deemed "open markets" where the licensee can sell books, but without exclusivity. This approach is well known in publishing but less so in the film industry. Distribution of completed films may be divided by territory but the original rights owner traditionally comes close to making an assignment of everything, holding back only stage and live television rights, which in turn may be subject to seven or ten years of restriction and a later first refusal on their exercise. Authors in this medium may also succeed in reserving sequel (if not re-make) rights. Industry patterns differ, but exclusivity is always a key point. As earlier suggested, EC law needs to be watched carefully since exclusivity may become its target.

Implications of "Best Efforts"

A less visible but important concept is the degree of effort required by licensees. Obviously the grantor wants a pledge of "best efforts" (American) or "best endeavours" (British), especially if the grant is unprotected by time limits, but the licensee's goal is freedom from standards of accomplishment. Here a subtle problem arises because in some jurisdictions an obligation to do something useful may be implied even if unsaid. For this reason, the absence of best efforts provisions may lull producers and publishers into a false sense of security. They should negotiate either for a clause explicitly disclaiming any obligation to engender royalties, or at least language such as "the exclusive right but not the obligation" to exploit what has been put in their charge. "The right but not the obligation" should become standard phrasing, and where "exploit" offends lay sensibilities, "turn to account" goes just as well, but sounds gentler. Some contracts go further, disclaiming implied obligations in long paragraphs instead of cryptic phrases.

Trademark Considerations

Then there is the trademark side. Wherever trademarks are involved, American law requires quality control for effective licensing and sometimes to avoid forfeiture of the mark itself. Disparate ownership country to country is another problem, but media contracts often ignore trademarks altogether. Only with merchandising tie-ups do these valued symbols share prominence with copyrights. That they deserve better is quite clear if only because trademark elements may survive copyright in the same work. The catch is that they are governed by different rules and cannot, for example, be as freely assigned without the goodwill they symbolize, or licensed without quality control as one does with copyrights. These at least are American principles, but different rules and different registries will distinguish trademarks from copyrights nearly always. Copyrights are more identified with the communications industries but a good question to ask oneself is whether the database or textbook or other copyright has a name that can earn its own living as a trademark.

Options

In the media, most rights acquisitions are done on option. The "buyer," or licensee, ties up the property for a year or two while seeking financing or other arrangements. Failing this the property reverts, but three interesting questions arise: first, who owns the derivative material written or the pilot recorded during the option period; second, whether the option clause encompassed the right to make adaptations and pilot films; and third, whether options can be structured in the alternative. This third question is the most complex since licensees may be unclear which of various media has the best prospects, and therefore unwilling to foreclose alternatives by premature election. It may be possible to buy the luxury of changing one's mind by providing a front price for each medium with a time limit for its inclusion in the grant, coupled with a clause to the effect that choosing A does not preclude a later choice of B or C. The rights owner, however, may not choose to indulge Hamlet. In any event options are usually how things are commenced. The full rights grant should be all worked out and annexed, ready to take effect only if and when the option is exercised. Whether the option can be assigned, and if so, whether at a profit will be covered later in discussion of assignability.

Sample Provisions

Two sample grant of rights provisions follow. The first is something a buyer should find congenial, while the second is pro-owner, narrow and specific. Neither is suggested as a detailed form, California style, but each serves as a point reminder in shorthand. Adaptation from one medium to another is the assumed objective. When services are employed, as distinct from the transfer of property such as rights to an existing novel, there may be union restrictions on what can actually be acquired. Aside from union impediments, licensees must also consider local laws protecting authors. These things vary from country to country. Where they do not intrude, the licensee's appetite is unfettered except by the rights owner's bargaining position. Even such obscure points as what other works may be packaged or displayed with the licensed work, for example whether a family portrait may be displayed with rogues, can and sometimes should be spelled out in advance. So should any trademark elements, but those require special treatment in a later section.

Alternative A

A hereby assigns outright to B, B's successors and transferees, the copyright in and to the work entitled _____ _____ in all its extant and future versions, including without limitation its title, format, graphics, characters, registrations, renewals, underlying database and all its other extricable component elements with the exclusive right but not obligation, as between the parties, to publish, produce, create or authorize derivatives, alter free of any claim based on or similar to "moral right," combine with other material and sell, license, distribute and otherwise exploit worldwide in any and all existing and future media, in any form or language, together with the exclusive right to litigate against third parties for any past as well as future infringements. Insofar as the internal copyright laws of any jurisdiction may not recognize outright assignments of copyright, it is the parties' intention that this transaction be governed by the law of _____ _____ and that the nearest possible equivalent to outright assignment be the outcome if the internal conflicts laws of a jurisdiction not recognizing outright assignment prohibit or impede acceptance there of the recited divestiture.

Alternative B

"Television Rights," the subject of this grant, shall mean the exclusive right but not the obligation to effect in Japan once per year each for a period of three (3) years from the date hereof, a television broadcast of the Event as received via satellite or, at Licensee's option, with delayed transmission via a clean feed videotape recording (including a natural sound audio tract) delivered by Licensor no later than 72 hours after initial broadcast, together with the right but not obligation to interpolate Japanese commentary and commercial messages consonant however with highest standards of artistic integrity and subject to Licensor's reasonable advance approval of advertising and promotional material issued or authorized by Licensee for use in connection with the programming.

Chapter 6

WORKS MADE FOR HIRE

Another form of grant is not really a grant at all, but a fiction. This is the work made for hire, where the employer or someone commissioning the work automatically becomes the copyright owner if the facts fit statutory requirements. Major novelists are unlikely to write for hire, but others ranging from corporate employees to certain artists inhabit this category. The arrangement looks ideal from a company's viewpoint, pay once and be done with it. But for hire acquisitions can create many traps.

Does for hire ownership automatically pick up any U.S. renewal term? Does it extinguish the moral right, a subject too easily overlooked in this framework? Are for hire criteria satisfied according to Dutch law, for example, when a British technical publisher engages writers and editors in Holland?

Concerns of this kind, and the probability of frequent changes in the law, suggest taking extra care with so sensitive a device. Waivers of the moral right make good companions to copyright ownership. So do explicit transfers of American renewals if these endangered species are still involved, but here we come close to an assignment, and this inspires a further safety measure.

The further safety measure is nothing less than an outright

copyright assignment to back up the desired for hire structure. What if you got it wrong? How can you be sure of possessing all the required qualifications? A second protective line keeps you safer, language such as "To any extent necessary for implementation of the foregoing and for the outright vesting of copyright and all other right, title and interest in Dutchco, I hereby assign" etc. It can be argued that safety nets admit the possibility of falling, but most of us will be more comfortable with such things in place

"For hire" as a concept has implications that go far beyond drafting techniques. Court interpretations of business relationships that were inadequately documented may startle whole segments of the communications industries. Something of that sort was noticeable, for example, when the Supreme Court of the United States held that a particular work of sculpture was not within either of the two main "for hire" categories provided for in the Copyright Act of 1976.* The sculptor was neither an employee preparing the work within the scope of his employment duties nor an independent contractor fitting one of the statutory sub-categories for commissioned works. Accordingly this dispute over copyright ownership ended happily for the sculptor. The case is mentioned here, though, as a monument to the necessity, or at least the immense usefulness, of contracts. Had contracts been in place, an opposite result might have been reached or better still, nobody would have gone to court in the first place.

The for hire problem appears in a great many company-staff relationships. Do the editors own re-use rights? Can the Berlin news "stringer" or the learned contributor to a French medical journal obstruct republication in English? A few contract clauses are better than a lawsuit.

Community for Creative Non-Violence v. *Reid,* 109 S. CT. 2166 (1989), and see 17 U.S.C. §§ 101 and 201(b).

Chapter 7

THE TRANSFER OF FUTURES

Why future rights loom large will be apparent not only to the publisher tying up the author's next masterpiece, but equally to the tax planner removing a literary estate from some high tax jurisdiction to an area with palm trees. Assuming the transfer is lawful, one must consider whether a total assignment does the job or whether periodic transfers must succeed it as new rights arise.

Somewhere half buried in this matter is another problem, whether a transfer document designed as a license may be read as an assignment, or vice versa, and by what court, and where. Ambiguous partitioning of the rights may defeat one's purpose. However, with proper foresight, a number of problems can be anticipated.

Exactly what "future rights" will be transferred deserves attention. No single answer exists, but a division of future interests by category, nature and origin may point the way. Some examples follow:

a) Rights to prospective material not yet in existence except *in potentia;*

b) Rights in prospective material based on and derivative

of some existing work, and therefore in a sense, partly in existence;

     c) Newly arising rights in existing materials, whether the same rights come under new ownership or different rights are created, for example, by changes in the law; and inevitably

     d) Some combination of the foregoing.

A moment's reflection makes clear why identifying the particular future rights to be caught up in the transfer net is critically important. Wording such as "all existing and future rights" may cover, for example, derivatives not yet composed while inadvertently excluding renewals not yet vested. The first seems to define a new property, the second a new owner. It pays to spell out what was intended, keeping in mind the remote possibility that too ambitious a reach for futures may be struck down somewhere as being against public policy.

Very likely, depending on where you are, the transfer of future rights should stand up on its own, not merely as a promise to convey them requiring implementation. So we are told by distinguished theoreticians, but doubts linger. Even a simple publishing contract specifying copyright ownership in the publisher raises the question how it got there from the author without an assignment. Industry custom, perhaps, but is it really sound? How can you get from New York to Boston merely by consenting to go there? Conveyance by some vehicle seems an essential step for accomplishment of the journey.

To be on the safe side, one does best implementing commitments for the transfer of future rights with actual conveyances listing the cargo. There may be reasons to rely instead on the promise to convey backed up by a lawsuit for breach, but that seems advisable only to diminish risk that later transfers admit a residuum, something left over from the original transaction still in the wrong place. For example an original transfer, let us say for tax planning, might by its phrasing cover "all future rights of any nature," leaving no rights left in the undesired locale, but later transfers might be admission that some rights, at least, never escaped their original situs. This could defeat your purpose. Absent this particular concern, it seems best to be governed by discretion, transferring the new rights as they come into existence.

Magic carpets are unreliable.

Chapter 8

ENCUMBRANCES ON RESERVED RIGHTS

What the grantee cannot acquire may at least be restricted for a period of time so as to be non-competitive. Reserved rights made subject to such restrictions may collectively be referred to as "Dog In The Manger Provisions," although that seems a little harsh considering the need to protect one's investment (and one's investors) against being undercut by rival productions in different media. That would amount to an erosion of exclusivity, to forestall which we try blocking what we cannot acquire, Dog In The Manger or no.

Six main encumbrances are much in use, but two among these stand on the cusp and scarcely fit, namely the Option and the Mortgage. The Option is a standard acquisition device we looked at earlier on, a pick-up within fixed time limits at a prearranged price. Sequels are frequently subjected to this arrangement. A second encumbrance, not yet considered and not scheduled for long analysis here, owing to its relative infrequency, is the Mortgage. Occasionally a bank or distributor insists on assignment of rights whose development it undertakes to finance, holding the hypothecated rights as security. There the important thing is to spell out what precise circumstances will free the impounded rights, and to have in place the cumbersome documentation effecting their return.

Fitting more comfortably within the encumbrance category are four very popular impediments, the First Negotiation, the First Refusal, the Last Refusal and the Restriction.

A right of First Negotiation, weakling of the litter, is not even enforceable in all jurisdictions. All it amounts to is something such as "before disposing of such and such rights you will negotiate first with us for thirty days." Pledges of good faith sometimes enrich the promise, but not sufficiently to give it real teeth. Essentially the First Negotiation solemnizes what people doing business together might do anyway, and lays somewhat infirm ground for a lawsuit if the promisor goes straight to a competitor without the courtesy of offering the surprised ex-partner a fair shot. It may, however, slow down a rival to whom the obstructing clause has been disclosed.

In the publishing field there are editors, unblessed by law training, who write options as first negotiations and thereby achieve nothing. "The Publisher shall have an option on the Author's next work," that sort of placebo unfortified even by time limits, is little beyond a kamikaze right of first negotiation.

The First Refusal, sometimes paired with First Negotiation, is quite a different creature. This one has teeth, and whoever ignores it does so at great risk. A right of First Refusal is essentially a right to match somebody else's offer within a prescribed time after being notified of its terms. If you meet those terms, you win. The question, however, is what terms have to be met, since money is not always everything in these matters, and other concerns ranging from fidelity of production to effectiveness of distribution enter the mix as well. It helps to recite at least generally what sort of terms have to be matched, even if you narrow it only to "business terms" so as to rule out artistic considerations, or the reverse, but of course the more specific the better. "Including without limitation" helps protect against inadvertent omission here, as elsewhere.

What if the encumbering grantee declines matching a rival offer and finds later that the grantor and third party rival have come unstuck before contract? In some cases it can be provided that the First Refusal right revives and will apply next time and beyond, if that should happen again. In imagery much beloved at the Bar, one has a second bite at the apple. Carried along sufficiently, it becomes a right of Last Refusal.

Another standard encumbrance is simply the Restriction, prohibiting for a time period the use of reserved rights. In the film industry, for example, reserved stage and live television rights may be frozen for seven or perhaps ten years.

A final point to be made about encumbrances on reserved rights is one that arises mainly with the settlement of controversies. Two companies dispute the meaning or the administration of their license agreement. Lawyers work out a settlement, and the license agreement is called off. Counsel have carefully tracked and provided for every sublicense that rightly or otherwise survives the main license as it comes to an end. Sublicensees will pay direct to the original rights owner, the prime licensee will give warranties that there is nobody else "out there" to worry about, everything looks tidy for the great divorce. Only one thing may have slipped through the cracks: a First Negotiation/First Refusal on future product that ambiguously survives. Chances are, however, that future impediments will be eradicated by the court with all the rest of it, but why play risky? A phrase or two forestalls these unpleasantries. Even "Any and all express and implied options, liens, rights of first negotiation, first refusal and other preferences, encumbrances, restrictions and favored positions are herby extinguished" should dim unwanted prospects of hearing from your old colleagues again just as you plan embarking on arrangements elsewhere.

Through such measures, the Dog In The Manger is locked out. Looking at things from the other side, a flat Restriction topped off by a First Refusal when it expires helps protect your investment. Either way, spelling it out is worth some trouble. Whether encumbrances survive is a major point.

Chapter 9
CLEARANCES

Implicit in our analysis of rights transfers is an assumption that whoever transfers them controls in fact something to assign or license, and more often than not there is an assumption that the grant will be exclusive. That these expectations will not be disappointed requires the support of warranties backed by indemnification, human nature suffering as it does from certain frailties, and so it appears logical that the next cluster of points should be Warranties.

Sell something, warrant that you own it; that seems sensible enough. But how can you be sure of owning the rights you transfer? Even the author may put down a wrong foot if burdened with a collaborator, or if he incorporates somebody else's material.

How to Proceed

The following points, then, should be carefully considered.

- **Secure permission before, not after,** incorporating someone else's material in your own, or adapting it for a different medium in other material. That sounds axiomatic, but there are people who flout this rule and pay dearly later.

- **Be very careful about relying on someone else to effect clearances on your own behalf.** A British publisher decides on leaving it to the Americans to save legal fees. Or an American author looks to the publisher to sort out the permissions headache. Neither example evinces a focused and deliberate approach. The American publisher may seem to have secured whatever rights are necessary, but (as it turns out) only for its own purposes, and inadequately at that. Japanese language rights? They never came up. Television? It never occurred to them, especially if they have no share in audiovisual media proceeds. Then again, perhaps they had the foresight to clear film and television use of the material, but never worried whether there was an implied condition to effect theatrical release in cinemas before television so as to avoid spoiling a major market, a concern that could have been eased with language such as "in any sequence of the licensee's sole choosing." Worse still, American rights of Privacy and Publicity may require waivers where interviews and perhaps taped performances are the borrowed material.

Relying on others to secure the necessary clearances is dangerous. The final indignity will be when those you relied on secure the desired rights, but only to themselves, and nontransferable.

- **Your permissions and clearances should at least parallel your own grant of rights to transferees.** Consider the position in steps: a publisher authorizing use in New Zealand must itself acquire New Zealand rights; if Sweden has an option followed by a first refusal, the clearance of outside material must cover that possibility as well; and even if New Zealand is out of the picture, and Sweden has nothing, it will be useful to lock up rights greater than what is minimally required first time out, just in case New Zealand and Sweden come into it later. Something left over always helps.

Parallelism in this context mandates careful consideration of options and other potentials not encompassed in the first use. Otherwise a licensor may suffer embarrassment through inability to deliver, as contracted, for a second year what had been dutifully cleared for the first.

- **What if collaborators wrote the material sought for incorporation?** Legal scholarship takes you only so far, and then you need support from other quarters. Traditionally England's copyright law barred grants by one joint owner without the other's consent while America took the opposite view, but presumptions can be varied by contracts, and so they ought to be whenever collaboration exists.

Suppose one writer defaults on the time limit for delivery, or the other incorporates pirated material, should both suffer? Risks of this kind are best divided at the outset of collaboration, and so are rights, which will be of greater interest to someone clearing the material. Must both collaborators agree? Which one receives payment? And most difficult of all, what if there is something beyond the usual duo as with computer-assisted creations?

Here you need special care. Perhaps the company furnishing a whole package should be approached for clearance. Or else, a programmer or provider of data may own and control the desired rights. Plausibly there may be co-owners by internal arrangement, and any one proposing, for example, to blend this sort of product through interactive systems into a derivative hybrid will have at least two puzzles to work out: first, figuring out from whom the rights are to be secured and second, determining who owns and may use the composite. There might even be a third puzzle, deciding whether exclusivity attaches by "merger" clause so that A and B are debarred from use of their own underlying material except as blended in the joint derivative.

Another complexity concerns the country whose law governs in the absence of clear contracts. Outlandish as it seems, there may be places where computers are considered authors.

Sample Provision

Pulling back from that brink, we wind down our discussion of clearances with sample language that goes a little further than some releases do, but without running on to a length likely to frighten off potential signatories or to inspire demands for substantial payment.

> "I am pleased to grant you and your publishers and other transferees the exclusive right but not obligation to incorporate in your forthcoming book on Field Marshal X and in all its future editions translations and derivatives in all existing and future media including television, feature film and video cassettes, all or any portion of whatever X-related material I now or may later control, including personal interviews, diaries, photographs, correspondence with you, letters to and from X to you or others, copyright material in any form covering him and all related material whether existing or prospective, all with the understanding that you may alter, edit and abbreviate the material, couple it with other material of your choosing and use my name, likeness and recorded voice and visual performance at your discretion in connection with and separately from your project and its promotion. Exhibit A annexed lists examples but not the entirety of subject matter covered by this consent, and is not all inclusive.
>
> Mindful of your obligations to publishers and others, I understand of course that you rely on my right lawfully to grant these permissions, and that you may secure copyright in the book and its other versions in your name or in the name of your designees.
>
> I am happy to accept your offer of a free copy of the book in English, if and when published.
>
> This constitutes our full agreement, which may not be changed orally and is governed by the laws of New York."

Sometimes, of course, no clearance is necessary for the incorporation of outside material. If this seems too obvious to be worth mentioning, consider an American publisher wanting to quote Plato in the appendix to a book on politics. The publisher solicits counsel's opinion on whether some short quotes from a protected translation exceed Fair Use. If they do, somebody will have to pay. How much easier it would have been, with a little imagination, to use a classic English translation by the great Chancellor Jowett of Balliol, material long since in the public domain! That would have brought enrichment through borrowed prestige instead of impoverishment through payment of royalties, but not many people read classics now, even in English.

This seems rather a pity. Ancient classics have a practical side, as the example shows.

Chapter 10

RETROACTIVITY

Certain works can be rescued in special circumstances from the public domain and restored to copyright status. In effect, they are protected retroactively. If that happens, clearance of the rescued material becomes preconditional to its use. This notion is something of a shocker, and so we hasten to distinguish from normal circumstances those few but intriguing variants that make it conceivable. Indeed, it should be noted straight off that the most likely origin of this possibility is the Berne Convention.

Only spells of that potency could revive lost copyrights. Otherwise one would have to make new works out of old, Chaucer in modern English for example, to acquire copyright, and of course the Middle English original would remain public domain. The protection of new versions is not, however, what is to be addressed here. Neither is uncertainty whether a deceased artist's Peruvian or Greek estate, for example, should sign permissions for reproduction of his works on museum post cards. If one set of heirs were to prevail, that would not actually present a retroactivity issue. A closer case would be where a change of political regimen results in claims of ownership by the state or its new wards, but these preliminaries lead inexorably to Berne, which squarely puts the question.

Berne Convention

Article 18 of the Berne Convention allows retroactivity:

(1) This Convention shall apply to all works which, at the moment of its coming into force, have not yet fallen into the public domain in the country of origin through the expiry of the term of protection.

(2) If, however, through the expiry of the term of protection which was previously granted, a work has fallen into the public domain of the country where protection is claimed, that work shall not be protected anew.

(3) The application of this principle shall be subject to any provisions contained in special conventions to that effect existing or to be concluded between countries of the Union. In the absence of such provisions, the respective countries shall determine, each insofar as it is concerned, the conditions of application of this principle.

(4) The preceding provisions shall also apply in the case of new accessions to the Union and to cases in which protection is extended by the application of Article 7 or by the abandonment of reservations.

U.S. accession to Berne in 1989 led to or followed the removal of various technical preconditions to the securing of copyright such as certain requirements of notice and domestic manufacture. Both now are consigned to history's dust bin, but the Manufacturing Clause may have caught, for example, so illustrious a work as *The Screwtape Letters* by C.S. Lewis. Is *Screwtape* (apart from its trademark elements) public domain in America? If so, that indignity arises from non-compliance with requirements now outlawed. Berne comes to the rescue, *Screwtape* is saved, but recapture of copyright is not quite that easy. Congress said no retroactivity and that, it would seem, is the end of it.

Still, retroactivity has its attractions. Certain American films unprotected in one country or another might be reinvested with copyright on some basis of reciprocity as the property of new members of the Berne club. Even the old argument that once in the public domain means you stay there forever ignores the possibility of provisional public domain status suggested long ago by a leading copyright expert.* This is not the place, however, to argue the legal aspects of retroactivity. Our concern is with media contracts, and on that subject there is plenty to worry about before reviving even a few lost copyrights.

The real problems are business concerns. Somewhere out there, working hard in the communications industries, people have invested funds and efforts on the legitimate assumption that certain works are in the public domain. Suddenly to be told otherwise is unthinkable if you leave it at that, nearly as unthinkable as new tax laws upsetting structures created lawfully in the past, but condemned now with retroactive effect. Surely some "grandfathering" is required. This perhaps is where Berne scholarship stands weakest. International law considerations eclipse what may be the weak link in retroactivity: protection of business investments undertaken in reliance on the absence of copyright. It may be helpful to imagine a few more examples of misplaced reliance than current writings on the subject disclose.

The main point is that things are infinitely more complex now than when Berne was young. At that time, newly adhering signatories could protect publishers by letting them print and sell the balance of an edition begun before copyright got in the way. An 1870 German law, for example, listed exemption from retroactive protection: "existing copies could continue to be sold; commenced publications could be finished; instruments such as molds, plates, cliches, etc. could continue to serve for the making of new copies until such time as such instruments could not longer be used." Moreover, the continued circulation of copies made before the coming into effect of the Convention was permitted publishers in Germany and Czechoslovakia confronted with unanticipated translation rights to works by Strindberg, Zola and Karl May.**

---

*(Bogsch, *The Law of Copyright Under the Universal Copyright Convention,* Leyden and New York 1968) at pp. 84–5.

**Those interested in further exploring these earlier exemptions should browse I. Ladas, *The International Protection of Literary and Artistic Property,* Chapter IX, p. 343 et seq. (New York 1938). For British and European analysis one may consult Rickelson, *The Berne Convention* (Queen Mary College and Kluwer, 1987), and various publications of the World Literary Property Organization in Geneva.

Problems of Reliance

Nowadays letting publishers finish out runs in progress is no longer good enough as the twentieth century draws to an end. Retroactivity problems nearly defy solution because so many transactions are undertaken world-wide in reliance on the non-subsistence of copyright. The sample instances of reliance sketched out below will have to be dealt with before retroactivity is made part of any major copyright system. In each case, the Reliant is whoever reasonably relies on the understanding that what would otherwise be intellectual property is in the public domain, and whose continued use of it would become an infringement if retroactive copyright applied.

- An author spends years adapting some public domain work for a different medium only to be barred suddenly from its use. In this example, unlike those that follow, the victim is not a big company but an individual and fellow artist;

- The Reliant commits to publishing a paperback edition, revised editions, translations, dramatizations, game books, answers to questions and sequels, suffering the same jolting interruption as will happen, too, in our remaining examples;

- The Reliant licenses film, television, videocassette and other subsidiary rights;

- A database is stored for computer, anthology and other use;

- Diaries and other family records are purchased;

- Research is commissioned;

- Premises are rented;

- Travel is undertaken;

- A novel is optioned with hopes (but no commitment as yet) for dramatization;

- Painting or sculpture is bought partly in expectation of reproducing it on posters;

- Lyrics for music are commissioned;

- An old film is colorized (there has been enough controversy in this area even with films clearly in copyright);

- Insurance issues on the assumption no clearance of literary material is needed;

- Distribution commitments are blocked in the territory where retroactivity is laid on;

- Tax planning is upset;

- Characters from children's books are entered in a parade float (trademark aside);

- A synchronization license to use music in a film sound track is issued for somebody's adaptation of what was thought to be an Andean folk tune in the public domain.

Note that damage results even where the Reliant has not yet committed any resources in reliance on copyright non-subsistence. Often there is no commitment down the line, and no contract to be thwarted. Instead, there is only a plan, a dream, or even a dim expectation. Nevertheless, this very consideration will have affected the purchase price. Surely the Reliant would have paid less (or kept out of it completely) if copyright clearance had looked essential. Retroactivity should never trap the innocent Reliant.

But where should reasonable expectation be cut off? Obstructing contract commitments is one thing, creating disappointment quite another. Should exemptions from retroactivity be available only when knots actually have been tied? Must one actually have spent money or made contracts to qualify for exemption? These questions are not only for intellectual property scholars. They deserve industry attention, with emphasis on fair ground rules balancing new rights against commitments and expectations. Perhaps a tribunal or ombudsman structure could help balance each side's interests case by case.

Perhaps too, this is all premature. Retroactivity creates a great many problems, and the United States, at least now, is having none of it. English and Swedish beginnings at Reliant protection offer only a first glimmer of light.***

Nevertheless, Berne and foreign trade considerations are not so easily swept away. They haunt the ramparts and command respect. It seems prudent to anticipate their arrival, not to dismiss these questions as otherworldly.

In world markets that allow retroactivity, its impact on clearances is vivid. Very simply, there will have to be more of them. New rights will require new license permissions unless in some exempt category. That in turn leads from the preceding discussion of Clearances to the next section on Warranties. If there is the remotest possibility of retroactive copyright, you will be especially careful in what you warrant.

Again, retroactivity would at best attach only to properties of a certain class. Even with such limited application, however, the stakes may be high, and those who go ahead innocently need some degree of protection. Otherwise the lost copyright may look like Sleeping Beauty while asleep, but wake up ugly.

***See *Geller, supra,* Introduction § 4[a][ii] footnote 517.2.

Chapter 11

WARRANTIES

Two maxims are nearly invariable, first, that nobody ought to buy rights without warranties and indemnities, and second, that insurance coverage should be explored as part of a more theoretical risk analysis. Both maxims are fundamental but frequently ignored. By one of those little ironies that infest copyright law, media people who fancy themselves "practical" miss out on the fundamentals. Some will rent film clips on the suppliers' forms without any warranties. Others produce programming without even soliciting premium quotes for "errors and omissions" insurance covering libel, copyright infringement and certain related claims. Buying a summer cottage inspires greater care. There nobody rushes forward without a title search, warranties and indemnities, proper insurance and other procedures taken for granted with tangible subject matter. Incorporeal property, somehow, puts the buyer off guard. Yet here, if anywhere, elaborate caution is essential. Warranties and insurance are where to begin when risks replace rights as the focus of attention.

What sorts of things should be warranted? Here are some that are most frequently encountered:

- **Freedom lawfully to make the agreement** (and to grant the rights granted, a quasi-redundancy). People sometimes forget or even ignore being tied to somebody else, and hence barred from other commitments, through some earlier exclusivity provision, a non-compete clause or a first refusal.

- **That the material is free of infringing, libelous and other unlawful matter** including violations of Privacy and Publicity rights. This example, like the one that preceded it, is a natural for cross-warranties and indemnities from a publisher or producer engrafting new material onto the original supplier's, or changing the original. The original supplier, such as an author, must take care to avoid inadvertently giving away greater alteration rights than intended when securing cross-warranties for alterations.

- **Copyright status,** such as recitals that a work is protected by copyright in the United States (traditionally the trappiest major market) and countries adhering to the Universal Copyright Convention and the Berne Convention. Some inexactitude results since Berne, for example, appears in successive versions and is subject to particular reservations distinguishing one signatory from another. But nearly anything is better than saying a work is in copyright "throughout the world" unless the promisor is the world's leading copyright scholar armed with up to the second status reports. "Throughout the world" actually appears in professional documents. It never should.

- **That no statutory reversion or recapture of the rights is possible,** but here again even the most learned scholars will be unsure, and this supplement to the status warranty may be too much to expect. More detail can more reasonably be ferreted out through recitals of publication date, registration and other specifics. Incidentally titles, inhabiting, as they do, the trademark area, usually are exempted from assurance of protected status, or at least of exclusive ownership.

- **The absence of adverse claims, tax liens and other impediments.** This one requires little comment except to note that world markets are at least potentially involved. If

there is trouble in Thailand, let it be smoked out for evalua-
tion.

- **That all necessary clearances have been secured and are currently in force.** Earlier however, we considered how inadequate many clearances may turn out when new uses of the material are planned, so that inspecting the releases yourself (without prejudice to the warranties covering them) is often prudent. This is especially true when commentary, music, graphics and other such elements are warranted, as they should be, along with the basic material.

- **That no royalties or other residual payments to third parties become due upon further uses of the material.** This is quite a separate matter from representations that one may lawfully publish or exhibit something. Acquiring the rights is only part of the problem. Payment of suddenly disclosed entitlements to writers or others possessing earlier contracts may bury the whole enterprise in costs. Indeed, a pick-up of completed films is especially vulnerable to these kinds of revelations. Consequently, all third party payment obligations should be listed in exhibits and backed up by warranties of completeness and accuracy, for even agents and finders may suddenly assert claims. It is vitally important to spell out in the main agreement how all of these obligations are to be divided. Nobody can do this, however, without knowing whether such obligations exist, and what they are. Warranties and representations from the side that knows (or ought to know) make the division of responsibility possible. Indemnification is the price for getting it wrong.

- **That no competitive rights were previously granted, even if no longer outstanding.** This is another area with rich possibilities for unpleasant surprises. Someone planning a production in Venice could have been put off by disclosure of last year's production in Padua. Naturally, as with other deterrents, such events can be listed in exhibits once the buyer is protected by disclosure and warranties. The point is to know, if only to warn financiers in your own contracts for funding.

- **Accuracy and freedom from risk.** These are sometimes warranted with technical writing such as material on diet, or perhaps the making of explosives. Product liability is a lurking risk, but elaborate warranties in this area will not always be easy to get.

- **Freedom from any obligation to accord writing credits, or to respect any third party's "moral right"** against changes in the material. This concern with unknown outsiders to the transaction is similar to that dealing with residuals.

- **Assignability,** which is vital with pick-up transactions. Warranties of ability to enter into the agreement ought to cover the point, but spelling it out is better when B is relieving A of an entire corpus of material by others.

- **Going beyond general patterns,** anything specific and ambiguous may call for warranties outside the main lines. Suppose, for example, that the contracting parties both have inspected an old underlying license of production rights for Belgium but disagree on its interpretation. Warranties by a solvent grantor may break the ice. Again, a proposed database licensee may object to continued computer storage of the database by a rival whose license expired months earlier. The grantor's assurance that the material cannot be competitively used will go just so far before warranties are requested. This time, indemnification is not the ending; which side may or must sue, how costs and recoveries are to be divided and counsel selected—all of these procedures against a third party need sorting out.

Our dozen examples support at least one resolution, which is to take nothing on faith. There are the odd exceptions—trustees, for example, only can warrant their best knowledge of what a deceased author may have done—but in most cases the grantor makes careful warranties and then stands (not hides) behind them.

What if the circumstances make it impossible to secure full warranties that sound "too legal"? Often, that seems a good time for exit. Those intent on assuming the risk, however, can at least try for disarming language such as "we rely on your assurance that," followed by informal recitation of things about which they need assurance, hoping by this shorthand to accomplish some of what a fuller warranty would usually provide.

As to insurance, generalizations are difficult because policies differ. Whether coverage should be laid on as early as pre-production or its equivalent, whether it will be available only on a case by case basis and after the submission of a programming outline, how to find money for premiums, matters of this kind usually are taken up with specialist brokers. One point is clear, however, that an author should request coverage under the publisher's policy, and at no cost. This is a reasonable contract point, but things grow complex with "self-insurance" or when co-producers or co-publishers divide risks in some enterprise undertaken in common. As always, the point is to be aware of the problem so that negotiation may bring about a solution.

Warranties and representations seem the dark side of trafficking in world rights. The very sight of them dims pleasure in the voyage, but this is true of life rafts and other measures that promote survival. Only the reckless will sail without them.

Mention of survival suggests a final point here, that warranty obligations usually survive the expiration of contract. When that is the intention, a clause saying so is worth composing. Things may go wrong years later, and it will be pleasing (unless you are the one who indemnifies) to dig out the old contract, and find yourself still protected.

Chapter 12

RIGHTS TRAFFICKING BY PROXY

Representations and warranties sometimes occur indirectly. When this happens, or ought to be happening, complex questions arise which elude easy solution.

Just as a commuter train, for example, takes on new passengers at successive stops, and the passengers present tickets for the journey, so a variety of rights may be pictured as being gathered on board, with warranties as the equivalent of boarding tickets. This gathering in stages subject to proof of entitlement looks straightforward enough, but if the railway changes hands there will have to be arrangements funneling proceeds to the new remote owner. How removed from its passengers, and how invisible behind the intermediary the real owner should be, is the riddle.

In the media one finds analogies in many transactions. Subdistributors of audiovisual product, a training film on how to play golf, for example, stand between the owner and its customers. The owners are in Scotland; unexpectedly some commentary supplied by Japan for its own version catches on, becomes valuable. Can Scotland use it? What rights did the Japanese subdistributor acquire from its commentator? Japan may be willing, but are those rights cleared?

The merchandising industry is where these problems most

frequently arise. This is so because the intermediary here, whoever arranges licensing for the commercial tie-up, often has
power to bind its principal, even to manufacture the licensed
articles itself in some cases, and therefore functions as half agent,
half licensee. The resultant hybrid contracts with sublicensees on
its own signature, and now the problem begins taking shape.
Who owns the successive input of sublicensees? Owner A invests
representative B with authority to bind A with C, who creates
derivatives. Who owns them?

Obviously A should. The underlying owner pays its agent a
good whack, more than literary agents can expect, and the
percentage payments without any transfer of rights should take
care of everything. Similarly with manufacturer C at the end of
the line; profit, not the acquisition of intellectual property rights,
is its goal and reward. Only A should own everything new as well
as old, absent special arrangements which of course can upset all
dogmatic pronouncements.

But how do the new rights get from C to A? B stands in the
way, collecting them all in its own vacuum cleaner, so to speak.
Differing formulations exist:

- Owner A provides in its contract with "agent" B that all new
  rights arising from third party contributions will belong to
  A, and there may even be some anticipatory assignment
  form annexed to the agreement;

- As above, but for greater protection an agreed form of
  sublicense with C is annexed to the contract between A and
  B and A's consent is required before it can be modified;

- A contracts direct with C, relegating B to agency status, or
  at most co-signatory.

A glance at these alternatives discloses that the first is
inadequately policed, while the third exposes the original owner
to contract privity that may be impractical, and to liability on
direct warranties that may be unwelcome. The second looks best
for most transactions. It shields the owner in some degree, but
maintains control. Thus a European rights owner may invest its

American agent with power to conclude merchandising contracts, but only on condition that an approved form be used, and that the approved form capture ownership from the sublicensee's creative artists, perhaps as work made for hire. The European owner may actually be named as a third party beneficiary and ultimate transferee of new rights, but without co-signing the actual contract for manufacture of food, or toys, or clothing. That way everyone is on notice but the opposite poles keep their distance.

Needless to add, perhaps, Europeans are not the sole rights owners who may find this approach workable, and the suggested formula can be varied to fit different business requirements. Approval of contracts with third parties is the common denominator. Rights owners will regret trusting intermediaries to sweep up new rights into the correct hands. Holding them to account on approved forms is the best security. Thus, if the manufacturer known as "C" in our complex trio should want basic terms changed, even a clause altered, back to headquarters the request must go, and "A" makes the decision.

A final point here is that sweeping up trademarks is trickier than garnering new copyrights. For one thing, spotting the new device that has trademark potential is like casting a new show. Nobody can be sure which performer has star quality. For another, trademark assignments require the accompaniment of "goodwill" as seen earlier, so that the entire exercise of conveying embryo assets from C to A is a little cumbersome. Still, trademarks have to be lifted into the right container. You never can be sure that somebody at the end of the line will not devise, and beat into the public consciousness, a new character, catch phrase, design or musical signature that has selling magic.

Let the magician's hat be your own. Of course with Soviet or other material from disparate legal systems, the chain of ownership may be hard to follow. The effort, nevertheless, may prove rewarding. Cut out all intermediaries as new rights arise. Pay them fairly but own everything and keep control.

Creative intermediaries may look at things a little differently. Perhaps anyone making a real contribution can let go its ownership but charge for its use when combined with the original work on which it was based. The composite, however, is derivative and rarely available for actual use by the contributor except on option, and when this happens, "C" becomes "D" and turns producer or publisher. The manufacturer, too, may engraft something original enough for claims of ownership.

Every link in the creative chain may be valuable. Their ownership and control as between distant parties requires thoughtful partitioning.

Chapter 13
A DUE DILIGENCE EXERCISE

Surely by this time, it may seem reasonable to expect, the subject of money would be exalted here by grave and respectful discussion. After all, payments are what the whole thing is about, are they not? Actually they are not; fame, reputation, artistic pride and other intangibles loom large in the media. Money is vital, but not the entire story. Then too, there is a structural reason why payment formulas are deferred here a little longer. The reason is that concepts of rights and risks need to be nailed down first; it would be illogical to consider payments without asking about what they are payments *for*, and to develop that point, almost certainly, media contracts postpone royalty and net profits clauses until nearer the end after the grant of rights has been delineated. Warranties admittedly come even further along, but that may be psychological, since these invariably sound unpleasant and their composers may be hoping subconsciously for inattention. In this book they were promoted to earlier rank as the dark side of rights. Accordingly we defer treatment of financial terms pending one additional exercise.

To review some main themes heard now from different sources, let us consider the American launching of long suppressed writings from Czechoslovakia. Assume them to be political dissents combining satire and cartoons with accounts of invasion by Third Reich and later by Warsaw Pact armed forces. Publishers bid for the corpus of material; television stands ready to leap in; and reflecting that spirit of enterprise which gladdens consumers everywhere, the merchandising industry plans a sale of Czech freedom trinkets, just as pieces of the Berlin wall were packaged and sold earlier when that edifice was dismantled.

How will its protectors and licensees approach this formidable material? A little detective work comes first. Corporate lawyers call it "due diligence;" you look into the position closely so as to make reasonably sure that things are in order, and to protect yourself against criticism if you find they are not. In media transactions the detective work is especially complex.

The main questions to be addressed are set forth below:

- **What exactly are the writings and their component elements** including titles, characters, photographs, interviews, cabaret sketches, recurring locales and other devices, formats, series and sequels as well as cartoon graphics and theme or other music from any media besides books?

- **To what extent is any outside material incorporated in the writings** owned by other Czech or foreign creative artists, and by what documentation have their rights been cleared at least in a degree parallel to our own proposed new uses including not only the territory "America" but the rights to alter their contributions free of droit moral, to combine their translations with others, and to control sequence of presentation?

- **Are there any obligations to third party contributors** to pay residuals for additional uses, or to accord name credit in a certain way, or to do or refrain from doing anything else that may prove a sudden impediment?

- **Are such third party rights exclusive, assignable and properly warranted** so as to ensure at least that the proper authority or owner is granting the necessary permission?

- **Can any outside material not satisfactorily cleared be excised without damage to the artistry,** or must we negotiate new deals, for example, commissioning new translations?

- Returning now to the basic works, **what are their respective histories world-wide in all languages and media** including original publication dates anywhere, whether the original publications bore the "c" in a circle, all publications and productions to date, and currently outstanding licenses or obligations surviving from old licenses such as rights of first refusal or options to extend territories and share foreign revenues?

- **Are there any trademarks or other registrations anywhere in the world?**

- **Are there any known adverse claims or restrictions anywhere** by government authorities, alleged collaborators or others?

- **Which fictional characters thus far seem the most commercially valuable,** and in which literary and graphic depiction?

- Since every license negotiation should be tailored to client preferences, representatives ought to know **which among the following the author most treasures** perhaps in disproportionate degree: cash up front, long term royalties, lawful tax minimization, money abroad, script approval or some more realistic assurance of artistic integrity, personal image, provisions for family, a political cause, free travel or some other objective whose sudden disclosures at five minutes to midnight may disrupt contracts nearly concluded, and shock their negotiators.

- **Have changes in Czech or Slovak political regimes affected the position?**

By pressing for answers to such questions you should get at least a feel for the property and a rough profile of its status.

Then, almost certainly, special problems will be revealed and explored. The due diligence exercise is essential for trafficking in media rights.

Omitting it is like buying a haunted house for resale.

Chapter 14

PAYMENTS

The ongoing payment stream rather than a single purchase price characterizes the media. There are plenty of exceptions arising with anything from the settlement of claims to a designer's fee, but new payments for additional uses are the norm. A few unofficial definitions with brief commentary will outline the main forms of compensation:

- **Royalties** typically are an entitlement to agreed percentages of box office receipts or of retail or wholesale prices for books, videocassettes and other recorded communications;

- **Residuals** are additional payments based on and constituting percentages of original compensation, as with television network repeats or post-network syndication, made sometimes in accordance with or to reflect union scales for successive uses;

- **Shares of gross proceeds** refers to agreed percentages of receipts off the top without any deductions, but the term is something of a misnomer since even with media such as the live theatre, where royalty compensation is computed on box office collections, there are standard deductions varying from one industry and country to another;

- **Net profits** are the divisible remainder after deducting all or part of a variety of elements ranging from agency commissions and local taxes to production and distribution costs, allocable overhead and shares payable to third parties who stand ahead of or *pari passu* with the participant. The skill of Hollywood studios in listing deductible elements is of course legendary.

These four modes of payment (five if you count flat fees) usually are backed up by accounting provisions for periodic statements and audit rights. Entitlement to copies of sublicensees helps the rights owner keep track of whatever is going on, and some owners insist on penalty clauses punishing errors in accounting. This last device is useful occasionally but exemplifies bad value judgments by owners who would rather hold out for something they understand than get the grand structure of controls and payments arranged to best advantage. In fact it may be said generally that even professionals sometimes focus on the wrong point, scoring triumphs with accounting procedures at the expense of identifying all of the potential money sources. For that more ambitious attempt, although nobody must make light of accounting details, one looks back to earlier sections on the grant and reservation of rights in copyrights and trademarks.

Tracking Sources of Payment

How do the various payment modes actually operate? Defining them is one thing, but they must be shown at work.

A first point is to provide in the contract for payment out of all sources, direct and indirect, "including without limitation" if specifics increase comfort. This sounds fairly simple and in fact it may be so if you are dealing, for example, with film distributors who in a particular case put up none of the production financing. The distribution agreement will cover the usual term and territory, furnishing of prints and responsibility for uncollected payments besides percentages for distribution fees, all on the distributor's form contract with amending riders. One such rider might call for payment to the rights owner when the distributor collects, not semi-annually, but that looks to acceleration of tempo rather than to the identification of sources. The main thing is to spell out all of the places and media where divisible compensation arises. Royalties for BBC "videograms" would be payable out of receipts throughout licensed territories. Additional compensation for "simulcast" via radio or high-definition television (HDTV) also may be shared with the rights owner. As always there will be exceptions, nothing for a Denmark or Greece, if special reasons exist, or half the usual percentage for pay cable, but exceptions can be recited without prejudice to the rest of it.

Distribution, then, requires no special imagination for the tracking of all money sources. All payments received "directly or indirectly during or after the term of this agreement for or in connection with the licensed property" is the sort of source-tracking language that makes it harder disguising exhibition receipts as non-divisible consultancy fees, but there is no special reason for the anticipation of dishonesty in this field and the rights owner may be better served by concern with currency conversion rates when foreign receipts are anticipated.

The tracking of payment sources grows more complex when we put aside distribution of recorded product and look instead at the programming itself. A single example suffices: suppose your company finances or furnishes material to a new festival of the arts in North Wales called *Caernarvon 2000*. Your contract looks very strong. You share in everything, tapes of the broadcast, souvenir books, even receipts from refreshment stalls on the festival premises. Best of all, you have options for the next five years. Then suddenly, the bad news is announced. Your festival is moving next year to the Black Forest and its new name is *Baden-Baden 2001*. The format is similar but protected by copyright, if at all, only by a hair (under whose law is another question). Do you share in the German festivities? Is Baden-Baden some sort of derivative work?

Litigators might find this an attractive case, but imaginative contract drafting should forestall their involvement. At least it seems worth a try ... "the arts festival known currently as *Caernarvon 2000* and all its severable component elements including without limitation the title, format and rights to works commissioned for performance at the situs, together with any and all derivative and other similar events presented anywhere in the world, under the same or a different title, by substantially the same management or with substantially the same sponsorship or artists at any time within the next five years." Undoubtedly that could be improved, but of course the festival authorities would have something to say about this, perhaps not all of it complimentary. Nevertheless it shows what can get away from you by changing form. No legitimate source of payment is too outlandish for contract identification.

Rates of Payment and Adjustments

So much for the ferreting out provision; we look next at what happens when the royalties actually begin flowing. They reflect variable rather than constant percentages under the terms of many contracts in the media. Sometimes the rate varies with performance: get on the best-seller list and your percentage rises; fail to "sell" Egypt within three years and your rate falls; one television special within a year keeps you level, but a series of at least thirteen half-hour episodes triggers an increase based on the number of households viewing in named market areas. Sometimes, however, the rate varies according to the number of copies sold, or perhaps arbitrarily with the passage of agreed time.

Calculating Net Profits

A third point concerns net profits. Some of the usual deductions before these are reached have been mentioned earlier, and there is no way every studio or publishing list of layer upon layer can be summed up in one place. Instead, consistent with a search for key patterns, we look at one trap that has caught even professionals who look at numbers but not at the concepts behind them. Suppose a production company offers a television writer a share of the net profits besides royalties and residuals. The usual deductions appear, production costs, distribution fees and other familiar items, and then the writer gets ten percent of the producer's net profits based on what remains. The arrangement looks fair, but this is an optical illusion. The producers, almost certainly, will have to give away half or more of their net profits to financiers. Assuming they contract away half, that leaves only fifty percent as the residuum on which the writer's share is based. Actually, then, the writer gets five percent of net profits, not ten.

An even worse case afflicts the author who may have heard somewhere that six percent, perhaps, is a proper royalty in merchandising. That may be all very well, but if some intermediary company stands between the author and manufacturer, the intermediary may get the six percent because the intermediary is the author's contract source here, leaving the author with six percent of six percent. These prospects are disagreeable but can be avoided by specifying the agreed percentage and then adding that the share is in no event to be less than a certain fraction of one hundred percent of net profits or royalty. That way, the producer or other intermediary suffers the loss for giving away too much to others. Similarly the rights owner should prohibit cross-collateralization where the licensed property is mingled with others in accountings, and its own figures are dragged down by unwanted company.

One must be aware also of those standing nearer the top of the payment hierarchy. Perhaps it will be a financier recouping double its investment, or an agent or obscure relative getting a finder's fee, or a key editor or director. Phrases that allow third party entitlements to come off before your own do can be dangerous or desirable, depending on where you stand. However it turns out, position in the hierarchy can make all the difference.

Revision Responsibility and Diminution of Royalties

Publishing agreements frequently contain clauses requiring revisions by the author when legal, medical and other technical material is involved. Updating the book is important but the standard terms offered by many publishers on this as on other points are unacceptable. Typically there is no additional advance against royalties. Many authors can live with that, but the small print goes on to say that if the author will not or cannot do timely revisions, somebody else can, and the publisher will debit the original author's royalty account by the costs of a successor. Theoretically at least, this can bring the original author down to zero. Aside from the possibility of misattribution, where the Roman history student for example mistakenly buys a copy of Gibbon's *Decline and Fall* rewritten by Marxist academicians, the original author and the author's estate are cut out even if the revisions are minor.

There are various ways to forestall this result and essentially they come down to provisions that the original royalties cannot be diminished below an agreed minimum as long as the book remains in print. (Cross-indemnification covering the new material is a companion piece.) A related approach involves diminution of royalties in fixed steps, as well as recapture of rights if the book goes out of print. Unlimited diminution of royalties is intolerable, and even when sensible limits are worked out, the original author must of course be offered the first opportunity at revision with protection of name attribution as well as royalties if somebody else does the update. It may appear that this publishing point belongs with earlier discussion of how royalties rise and fall according to varied circumstances. In a sense it does, but a new element supports its separate treatment here. The new element is the burden of more work by the rights owner just in order to stay level. That burden, admittedly, is not taken up in these hypothetical revision quandaries, but the very fact of its intrusion, and the greater likelihood of an author's inability rather than unwillingness to carry it, make limitation on payments for outsider material a point all its own. Diminution yes, but without limitations, never.

Financing

We need to say a few words about financing. Distributors and others who sometimes invest money in media productions share a number of concerns in addition to the expectations of profit. These include assurances of completion, protection against exceeding the budget, reasonable fiscal and sometimes creative control, and of course recoupment above all else. These aims are pursued through a variety of contract measures not actually in point here, but one reminder is useful in considering payment for rights. The financier stands nearly always as the potent but invisible puppet master in these affairs. No direct contract privity with the rights owner usually exists, but the financier's presence is there, even if a few steps removed. This distance element affects payment. Consideration for the rights may be coming ultimately from a cable licensee, or a film distributor, or a merchant bank funding the adventure. Somewhere along the way, the financing entity and the rights owner will come close without necessarily colliding. Perhaps C will guarantee A's royalties from B, or stand insatiably in the way of A's profit-sharing with B, or confuse everyone including the lawyers as part of a long international rights chain created for tax purposes. The possibilities defy enumeration.

What stands very clear is that direct contract privity is rarely the whole story. Somebody else is out there at the end of the chain. Awareness of each link helps ensure not only the protection of rights, but of payments too. We contract often with go-betweens, but keep sight of non-signatories.

Sophistication with matters of finance, it may be noted so as to balance these considerations, is not always an establishment preserve. Some years ago *Variety* reported that members of a pygmy tribe, fed up with being photographed by *The National Geographic*, were forming a union to negotiate for "residuals."

The genie is out of the bottle.

Chapter 15

ASSIGNABILITY

The ownership of copyrights and trademarks changes hands in quite different degrees of public visibility. At the top of the scale stand mergers and acquisitions where everything, or just short of it, comes under new ownership. Next in prominence would be sales of complete inventory where one publisher, for example, acquires another's catalogue but not its stock shares. Then there are the quieter bread and butter transfers that most concern us here because of their importance with media contracts. A few words on the subject are all it requires.

Unloading unwanted rights purchases on third parties or brokering them at a profit would seem normal expectations with property ownership. So they should be, unless reliance on the buyer's unique skills or greater solvency make the prospect of resale unacceptable. Still, in surprising degree, rights to assign are left out of informal contracts and are saved up instead for the boiler-plate that comes later. Sometimes this is safe, but it can also become unpleasant when you have to look up law at a future time to find out whether assignability is implicit. A contract phrase or two would have done the job, except where national law (subject to conflicts) impedes transfers.

Even letters of intent can compress an entire family of future assignees into phrases such as "you and your transferees" which may cover licensees as well. Better still, of course, is language of the sort devised long ago by the American television networks, which kept it short but foreclosed implied restrictions against partial or successive transfers: "We shall have the right to assign this agreement fully or in part at any time and from time to time to any person, firm or corporation anywhere in the world." Independent producers selling packages to the networks were usually able to append riders keeping the network liable if its assignee defaulted in payment, but were themselves constrained from assigning anything except the money proceeds derived from the transaction.

However it turns out, assignability is a key point that too many contracts leave up in the air. Vagueness in this area may obstruct transfers worth fortunes.

Then too, assuming they will be worth anything at all, the question of unconscionable profit arises even where assignability is clear cut. What if our friend B (promoted to buyer now from status as mere intermediary in earlier examples) resells A's former rights to C at ten times the cost? A, feeling hard done by, consults the precedents on undisclosed principals and related subjects only to find that most of them deal with real estate, and shed little light. Here too, there are ways of setting solutions in place. Assignment can be permitted, but not at a profit. Alternatively the contract may allow assignment at a profit but only on condition that any profit be split according to agreed percentages. The point is to work it out in advance.

Assigning trademarks, as shown earlier, raises special problems not encountered with copyrights. "Goodwill" must accompany American trademark transfers, and this element reflects fact even if embellished with a degree of fiction. You cannot simply move these assets about at will on the world chessboard. Consequently the tax planners sometimes need coaching on how to place all their pieces on the right squares.

As with copyrights, the best squares for them are not up in the air. Assignability plays a key role in media transactions. Silence on the point is unworthy of good contracts.

Chapter 16
THE COMMON MARKET

Long before "Europe 1992" the European Economic Community presented members and non-members with problems that inspired a vast legal literature all its own. One subject that attracted much attention was Intellectual Property. The Max Planck Institute in Munich, for example, published learned commentary on the *Coditel* case* where a Belgian licensee of the film "Le Boucher" succeeded in blocking retransmission of a German television broadcast via Belgian cable, notwithstanding Community policy against trade barriers. Non-members such as the United States worried out loud about business problems such as whether an American author should grant British and Commonwealth rights to the same publisher that got the U.S. and Philippines if restrictions against selling books outside the licensed territories were to be removed within Europe. Rights owners, distributors and collecting societies were affected by Articles 85 and 86 of the Treaty of Rome, setting the EEC course against the partitioning of markets. Transborder barriers were a target. The European Commission and the European Court of Justice offered plenty to think about for copyright owners. Division by language instead of territory and borrowing concepts from pa-

*See ECJ 12IIC207 (1981).

77

tent and trademark developments offered clues, but copyright was explored more slowly.

Later on, these complexities were enlarged by prospects of Community membership by countries in East Europe. For that matter there is no reason to confine attention just to Europe. Asia may develop trading blocs with their own rules, and within them new countries such as a unified North and South Korea may alter the landscape. Prediction is harder than ever, and just keeping pace is an accomplishment.

But why are these developments of such practical concern? The reason has been suggested earlier in this book, and becomes apparent if you step back a little from the complexities of contract and focus on the basic pattern of dealing with rights. It then appears that the underlying motif, the essence of the game, is the partitioning of rights into spheres. I get Germany but you keep France. Somebody else has first refusal on Spain, and as if division by territory were not enough, partitioning by medium and restrictions on the import of tangibly embodied literature such as books round out the establishment of copyright empires. Now it comes clear: this division into exclusive spheres seems the very thing against which the Common Market takes aim. Obviously there are distinctions, books as against television signals for example, but those in the firing pit have little leisure, and slender means, for keeping up. Intuition however, if nothing else, suggests the necessity for watchfulness. Nobody knows when or where the axe will fall, but if the worst happens, a supranational policy designed for the laudable promotion of free trade may cut into established ways of licensing copyrights. That may be a good thing geopolitically, but casualties attend the fall of empires.

How can the worst pitfalls be avoided by contract? Obviously one must take local advice and keep informed of developments. A few possibilities, however, may be usefully kept in mind for discussion with foreign counsel. The question is how to provide in contract against the possibility that partitions of rights, the very essence of the transaction, may be held illegal on challenge by a business rival or by the supranational authority itself. Here are some alternatives:

First, stick to your guns and ignore the problem. If your division of rights is held unenforceable somewhere, you can shop for a more congenial jurisdiction and sue for reformation, or frustration of contract, or whatever best suits the occasion locally. This ostrich approach, needless to say, seems impossible for Community members and unattractive for Americans and others outside the club. Perhaps ignorance may avoid being fined, but it offers too little.

A second approach is for the contracting parties at least to agree on jointly opposing any challenge to their arrangements. This way, with the division of costs worked out, the prospect of disappointment in how allies react is diminished.

A third way echoes *force majeure* and preemption clauses in a number of television contracts covering the obstruction of broadcasting. Obviously the prevention of rights partitioning is far worse in that the delay is permanent and the obstacles grander. Still, we have here a sort of *force majeure* resulting not from Act of God, but from ruling by the European Court or its equivalent. This being so, it may be sensible to provide that if the division of exclusive territories is overturned, the grantee whose turf is invaded is to receive fair compensation through the award of money, or of a less vulnerable territory, or perhaps another medium, or a combination of these elements, by an agreed arbitrator. Just how final and beyond the reach of appeal machinery the rejected rights partitioning must be is another question, especially if the adverse decree is challenged in a different country, but this may be a case where the rewards of harmony outweigh the difficulties of its attainment.

A fourth approach is to provide that the contract terminates completely (or in agreed respects) if the partitioning of rights is knocked out. Whoever goes this route may find restoration of the *status quo ante* unreachable. Accordingly this drastic an approach seems risky.

Discussion of these sample patterns with foreign counsel may suggest some hybrid approach, or inspire a new one, or make it unnecessary to cover these troubling points at all. However it comes out, exposing these formulas to local reaction should bring dividends. Then too, there is one crucial point that needs mention again, in this special context.

Whatever formula you choose, whatever pattern you explore with foreign counsel, remember that cut-off provisions may destroy sublicensees at the end of the chain. If A loses Italian rights, so may B, or even C in Poland or D in Japan. No man is an island. Arrangements all through the line have to conform instead of leaving D hanging when A's rights fall. Perhaps if that happens, D's country will refuse to accept that A's rights are lost because the European Court says they are, but terrible muddles result if arrangements are not co-terminous. Getting each licensee to agree on the same cut-off makes for hard contract negotiation, but the alternatives are worse. Logic, at least, supports some version of simultaneous rights extinction. Nobody, except in rare circumstances, can grant rights greater than those he controls.

Contract patterns, too, deserve unimpeded border crossings. What works in the European Common Market may succeed, with some local refashioning, in a new Republic, or a Pacific trading bloc. If the new sovereignty bars the division of rights into spheres, you and your contract partners will cope better if the prospect was at least generally foreseen, with alternative machinery laid in place.

The world's copyright systems are not yet harmonized. Until they are, transborder perspectives are indispensable.

* * *

Our trek has come a considerable way now, sometimes through exotic territory with its own folklore. Step by step nevertheless, the way becomes less unfamiliar. Patterns appear: look beyond national borders, look past the immediate contract signatories, be concerned with subsidiary rights, insist on warranties, beware net profits, spell out the rules for unloading what was earlier acquired. These and other principles apply no matter how many new technologies are devised. These are the rules, only there is another that stands higher, which is to know when they are to be broken or ignored. Dogmatism is out of place in the media. Disciplined imagination is the important quality because we never can predict what bit of scribbling may engender fortunes, or topple regimes by satellite.

Part II

Part II

SAMPLE AGREEMENTS

How sample agreements reflect or fail to reflect patterns outlined in Part I is examined in what follows. The samples are not necessarily suggested as models, although all of them have done actual service at one time or another. A different aim supports their inclusion here. They serve to show earlier assets full grown now, drawn out from the idea bank and introduced into the realities of commerce.

One of these realities is that we cannot always use maximum language to achieve our ends. The laity, people signing releases for example, suspect lawyers and bristle at law language; clients instruct their own counsel to go easy so as to avoid upsetting the other side; then euphemisms and short forms replace what ideally should be spelled out with uncompromising clarity, adding to the risk but perhaps saving the transaction.

An opposite reality is the disparate bargaining position where major companies insist on use of their own forms, hammering all their desired points with brutal prolixity. National legislation to protect the weaker side is not always an attractive solution either. Too much of it erodes free choice, and sometimes becomes a little patronizing.

Then there is the ultimate reality, that choice of law clauses are vital since many countries restrict what grantees can acquire.

Form A:
Short Release

FORM A: SHORT RELEASE

With my assurance to you that I am free lawfully to make this agreement I consent, for total compensation of _____ , to your unlimited and freely transferable uses in all current and future media, in any form(s) and language(s) anywhere as you designate from time to time, of my name and likeness, recorded performance(s), writings and other products of my services in connection with your cable series currently entitled _____ , and with all subsidiary rights in that series and its derivatives.

Comments

This form is inadequate for heavy duty but may be useful in circumstances where a program guest, for example, objects to signing anything at all. Its text, accordingly, abjures legal vocabulary wherever possible and comes out as a series of euphemisms. The idea is to cram as much as possible into a single sentence. Whoever signs it goes at least part of the way toward protecting the company. That half a loaf is better than none is an adage that fits many negotiations. The following points should be noted:

1) The "release" begins with a diplomatic "assurance" designed as a minimal warranty.

2) The "consent," coming next, is really a grant of rights, at least in part, and it may be useful to research whether any common law jurisdiction where forms of this kind are used requires payment of consideration.

3) The word "unlimited" before "uses" encompasses both space and time although naturally it would be preferable to spell out both.

4) Similarly, "transferable" covers both assignees and licensees.

5) Reference to "all current and future media" picks up new audiovisual devices as well as established carriers.

6) The phrase "in any form and language" is shorthand for rights to alter, translate and adapt.

7) The word "anywhere" sounds less formidable than "throughout the world."

8) Saying "as you designate from time to time" allows for changes of mind and the avoidance of implied sequences of use.

9) The "name and likeness" is American Right of Privacy waiver and its equivalents elsewhere.

10) Reference to "recorded performance(s)" covers fixation on film or tape or some other embodiment belonging, although the point is not spelled out, to the release beneficiary (or its transferees).

11) Now for a key point often overlooked, the word "writings," is designed to create the broadest feasible license for use of any preexisting or ad lib creative material conceptually separate from a personal appearance or name license.

12) Mention of "cable series" is only an example of identifying a property besides reciting its title, and in some cases may be best omitted.

13) Reference to "all subsidiary rights" is Faustian in its reach.

14) The phrase, "and its derivatives" lunges beyond new versions to more remote things, new properties based on the original. Armed with imperfect releases of this type you should at least have a negotiating position vis-à-vis signatories and something to show transferees.

The connoisseur will readily improve on the language of Form A: find better ways than "total compensation" to say "no residuals," substitute "compositions" for the ambiguous word "writings," disclaim any implied obligation to make use of the permissions granted, these and other enhancements are scarcely beyond reach even under the oppression of time pressure. Again, however, the suggested text is essentially a check list of points. Whether to include others, or to word even these more diplomatically, depends on balancing the risks in each unique setting. Perhaps even more can be crammed into a single sentence.

Form B:
Film Rights

FORM B: FILM RIGHTS

OPTION AGREEMENT

Address of Rights Owner   Date:

Dear _____:
    This sets out the entirety of our agreement, which is governed by the laws of New York and may not be altered except in writing signed by us both, concerning a literary or other work currently known as _____ _____("the Property") more fully described in the annexed Literary Purchase Agreement ("Exhibit A").

    1) For total consideration in the sum of _____ ($U.S. _____) receipt of which you acknowledge, you hereby grant to us, our assignees and licensees, the irrevocable and exclusive option, to be exercised if we so elect by furnishing you at the above address with written notice to that effect issued on or before 6 P.M. _____ time _____ 19 ___, to enter into and thus activate Exhibit A with you as "Owner" and us as "Purchaser."

2) Our option may be extended for an additional period of _____upon our furnishing you with similarly addressed notice to that effect issued on or before expiry of the original option period accompanied by payment of further consideration in the sum of _____Dollars ($U.S. _____).

3) The option payment(s) will be credited as an advance or as advances against first payment specified in ¶10 of Exhibit A if the option in the original or extended form is timely exercised.

4) During the option period(s) we may but are not required to create or commission the creation of one or more teleplays, screenplays or other adaptations of our choosing based on the Property, in any form or language for any medium with any writer(s) of our designation, and to record on tape or otherwise one or more derivative productions for "pilot" use, with the understanding that any resultant derivative will belong, as between us, solely to us notwithstanding their possible immobilization in the event we decline or fail timely to exercise our option(s) so that the underlying rights listed for transfer in Exhibit A remain unacquired.

5) Definitions of the Property in ¶2 and all your warranties and indemnities in ¶5 are brought forward and incorporated by reference as part of this Option Agreement but in all other respects Exhibit A, even if signed or initialled by either or both of us, shall not become binding or effective unless and until we signify by the furnishing of written notice our intention to exercise our option as above provided, and without that invocation Exhibit A reflects only contingent events and we are free of any express or implied obligation to exercise any option or to undertake or continue production once undertaken if we do ultimately exercise our option and make Exhibit A our agreement.

6) At any time and from time to time during the original and any extended option period and without

limit thereafter if Exhibit A becomes effective, we may assign this Option Agreement and Exhibit A to anyone anywhere on terms solely of our choosing provided only that we shall remain liable for payment of any contractually agreed compensation to you if our transferee defaults in the payment, and we shall be relieved of all potential liability whatever if our assignment or license is to one of the following:

7) You agree to waive, insofar as consonant with its implementation, any right of *droit moral* or its equivalent, and to cooperate at our request in the accomplishment of any copyright formalities permitted and/or essential for protection. Throughout the original and any extended option period you undertake to maintain, protect and avoid encumbering the copyright and any trademarks, service marks and other rights in the Property in every country where protection is available.

Agreed   Very truly yours

_____   _____

LITERARY PURCHASE AGREEMENT

AGREEMENT made this _____ day of _____, 19 ___, between _____ hereinafter (whether one or more) called the "Owner," whose address is _____ and _____ hereinafter called the "Purchaser," whose address is _____ .

1. The Owner hereby grants, sells, assigns, transfers and sets over unto the Purchaser, exclusively and forever, the entire silent, sound, dialogue, talking and musical motion picture rights, televised motion picture rights, television rights, audio-visual, cassette, disc and related videogram rights and dramatic rights (excepting only the right of production on the legitimate stage with living actors appearing and speaking in the immediate presence of the audience) in all languages and for the entire world, all such rights being hereinafter included in the expression "motion picture and allied rights," in and to certain literary and other material entitled _____ (hereinafter referred to as "the Property" and more fully defined below) written by _____ , hereinafter (whether one or more) referred to as the "Author."

2. "The Property" is identified as follows (delete whatever is inapplicable):

(a) Created originally in the form of a _____;

(b) Based on the following underlying material: _____ ;

(c) And first published in the year _____ and in the language: _____ ;

(d) Registered and renewed for U.S. copyright as follows: _____ ;

(e) Current trademark and service mark registrations of the elements in the Property country by country: _____ ;

(f) Licenses granted to third parties and other prior uses _____ :

(g) Existing film and/or audiovisual recordings, phonograms and other tangible fixations_____ :

The Property is hereby defined to include without limitation all its existing and future translations, adaptations, elements from third party material, real and fictitious characters, character names, titles, prefaces, notes, supplements, editions, logos, designs, illustrations, key phrases, sequels, formats, music and lyrics, recurring devices and other component elements and derivatives in any and every existing and future form, language, edition, version and medium.

3. The Owner agrees that included among the rights in and to the Property so conveyed are the following:

(a) The sole and exclusive right to make motion picture versions and/or television adaptations of the Property, or any part thereof, including sequel uses of the characters, and to produce one or more silent, sound, talking, dialogue and/or musical motion picture photoplays of any type now known or hereafter to be known, based upon or adapted in whole or in part from the Property, or any part thereof, or any such versions or adaptations (all such photoplays, versions or adaptations being hereinafter included in the expression "motion picture version");

(b) The sole and exclusive right to translate into all languages, freely to adapt, animate, change, transpose, revise, rearrange, add to and subtract from the Property, or any part thereof, and its title(s), theme, characters, plot, sequences, incidents and character-izations, to make interpolations in and substitutions for any of its segments, to combine with material by others, to make sequels to and new versions or adaptations of the Property or any of its segments, to make serials of the Property or any of its segments of two or more episodes of any lengths, to use any segments of the Property or of its theme or any

incidents, characters, character names, scenes, sequences or characterizations therein contained in
conjunction with any other work or works, to combine
episodes into a new unified work with or without new
materials, and separately or cumulatively to do any or
all of the foregoing to such extent as the Purchaser,
in its sole discretion, may deem expedient in the
exercise of any of the rights, licenses or privileges
herein conveyed and in the making of any motion
picture versions and other adaptations and versions
herein elsewhere mentioned; to interpolate in any such
versions or adaptations musical compositions, songs,
lyrics and music of all kinds, to set to music any verse,
lyric, prose or part or parts of the Property and any
characters thereof, and to use, print, reprint, publish,
copy or vend such song, the music and/or lyrics (sound
on film, magnetic tape, wire, record or other reproducing device, whether similar or dissimilar to the
foregoing, and whether now or hereafter known), on
commercial phonograms and otherwise, and to perform, whether or not for profit, to arrange, adapt and
exploit it or them throughout the world and to secure
copyright therein throughout the world in the Purchaser's name or otherwise, and to use, superimpose and/or
photograph lines, excerpts from or translations of the
Property for the title, subtitles, text and dialogue of
any motion picture versions and/or for interpolation in
motion pictures and other works in any medium not
necessarily connected with the Property or with the
Purchaser;

　　　　(c) The right to advertise, sell and exploit the
Property and its title or titles and/or other elements
and such motion picture versions and other adaptations and versions herein elsewhere mentioned, in any
manner and through any media and in any sequence
that the Purchaser may select and, for the purpose
thereof, to publish or cause to be published in any and
all languages and in serial or such other form as the
Purchaser may deem advisable, including publication
in newspapers, fan magazines and trade periodicals,
synopses, summaries, resumes and stories of the
Property and of any such versions or adaptations, not

exceeding, however, TEN THOUSAND (10,000) words in length, to use excerpts from and resumes and summaries of the Property in heralds, programs, booklets, posters, lobby displays, press books, newspapers, magazines and other periodicals, commerical and other tie-ups, and all other media of advertising and publicity whatsoever, and to secure copyright therein in the name of the Purchaser or its nominees;

(d) The sole and exclusive right to broadcast, by radio, wire or any other means or method, or license or authorize others to be broadcast, one or more radio adaptations, versions or sketches of any motion picture version, or of the Property, or any other adaptations or versions herein elsewhere mentioned, and any segments thereof, from disc or other sound records, sound tracks, tapes, electrical transcriptions, re-recordings or with living persons or otherwise;

(e) The exclusive, unlimited and unrestricted right to produce, issue, reproduce, remake, reissue, distribute, exhibit, transmit, project, perform, sell, lease, rent, license for exhibition, exploit, dispose of and generally deal in and with in any other manner or by any method whatsoever, whether now known or hereafter devised, and for any market, one or more motion picture versions, and trailers in connection therewith, including negatives and positive prints, of any size, color or type, and to secure copyright and copyright registration of such motion picture versions in all countries of the world in the Purchaser's name, or otherwise;

(f) The sole and exclusive right to make, copy, vend, license and otherwise use in any manner that the Purchaser may desire, disc or other sound records, sound on film, and any and all other mechanical, electrical and any other contrivances or devices of any nature whatsoever, for the recordation and re-recordation of the sound, talking, musical and any and all other audible portions of the Property (whether or not separately from any motion picture, as by a music "video") and any adaptations or versions thereof and any motion picture versions, or any segments of any of the foregoing, and for the reproduction, transmission, projection and/or performance of any or all such sounds separately or as part of or incidental to or in synchronization with the exhibition or performance thereof, whether such contrivances or devices are now known or are hereafter known, invented or devised;

(g) The sole and exclusive right, initially or at any time, to transmit, broadcast, project and reproduce the Property and any adaptations or versions thereof and any motion picture versions, or any segments of any of the foregoing, and/or the sound, talking, singing, and other audible portions thereof, through space for exhibition or reproduction at any and all places away from the originating projection source or to be performed, with living persons, fully or partly animated, with puppets, or otherwise, by television, radio, electrical transcription, electricity, facsimile or in any other manner or by any other method whether now known or hereafter known, invented, or devised;

(h) The exclusive right initially or at any time, whether or not one or more feature motion pictures shall be produced hereunder for theatrical release, to adapt and produce the Property or any of its component elements for any and all existing and future audiovisual media in any form or language and in color or black and white, with actors or puppets or animated, and thereafter to exhibit or license for exhibition, sale or rental the resultant pilot, special, motion picture for television, series, spin-off and other programming anywhere in the world via "free" network television, syndication, pay-TV, cable, pay-cable, satellite, video cassette, video disc, cinema theatres, ships and other vehicles and all other existing and future outlets, surfaces and media whether originating live, on film or tape or by any other method now known or hereafter devised;

(i) The exclusive right to publish or license for publication and sell in any form or language souvenir programs, cartoon strips and/or a novelization of each motion picture version or television program in English or any other language and in any part of the world; and to combine such novelizations with others as an anthology whether or not based on work by the Author;

(j) The exclusive right (insofar as the Owner can grant it) to use the title or titles and other identifying devices, in all languages and forms, by which the Property is now known or may hereafter be known, or any components of any such title or titles, or sub-titles, as the title of motion pictures, novelizations and/or programs and in connection with the advertising and exploitation thereof, whether or not such motion pictures, novelizations or programs are based wholly or partially upon the Property; and to use such title or titles and devices or any components thereof in connection with musical compositions and songs and with their publication, recordation, performance and any other use whatsoever;

(k) The exclusive right to secure copyright, trademark and other protection including registration of such motion picture versions, and any other versions or adaptations and characters and other component elements of the Property herein elsewhere mentioned, and any sound records, sound tracks, or recordings in connection therewith, in all countries of the world under any now existing or hereafter enacted laws, treaties, conventions, proclamations, regulations or rules, in the name and for the benefit of the Purchaser or any other person, firm or corporation the Purchaser may designate;

(l) The exclusive right to use and license the use of the Property, its characters, locales and other elements and their respective names, depictions and other identifying devices, with or without material by others, for commercial tie-ups in the merchandising field anywhere in the world in connection with any products and services, including without limitation their use or the licensing of their use for premiums and giveaway products, for theme parks, floats, for names of organizations and as "spokesmen" symbols for any product or service advertised on television and/or in other media, all with the understanding that the Purchaser or its designee shall own in its own name and may but need not register throughout the world, and will have or deputize the right to exercise quality control concerning, any and all trademarks, service marks and other protectible symbols arising anywhere from the Purchaser's exercise of its rights under this agreement or from use or registration or from any combination thereof;

(m) The right to use the Author's and/or Owner's name, likeness, pseudonym, sobriquet and recorded voice and image in connection with the Property and its promotion, but not as an express endorsement of any product or service;

(n) The exclusive right to submit productions based on the Property for awards at prize festivals and similar events, and to authorize their exhibition free of charge to the handicapped, the Armed Forces of any nation and other groups without limiting the Purchaser's exclusive rights to commercial distribution worldwide in all existing and future media.

The foregoing rights, licenses, privileges and properties may each be exercised independently of the others in any sequence and shall be held by the Purchaser, free of any claim arising under the *droit moral* or similar doctrine, throughout the world and the enumeration thereof shall not be deemed to restrict or limit in any way the generality of the grants herein made. Nothing herein contained shall be interpreted or construed to obligate the Purchaser to produce or complete any motion picture or other version of the Property, or exercise any of the rights, licenses or privileges herein conveyed. Certain rights however, not herein granted to the Purchaser shall be reserved to the Owner, subject to the right of first refusal and other restrictions as set forth elsewhere in this agreement.

All rights granted herein are transferred perpetually and irrevocably and are not subject to recapture under any circumstances except for any applicable statutory reversion properly invoked or automatically occurring at a legislated time. All the grants of characters, titles and other devices that may serve as marks include assignment to the Purchaser of all goodwill therein.

4. The Purchaser shall have the benefit of all copyrights and any renewals and extensions thereof in the Property together with all trademarks and service marks and goodwill therein, and all remedies for protecting such rights with reference to the rights herein granted, and the Owner hereby appoints the Purchaser the Owner's true and lawful attorney irrevocably, in the Owner's name or otherwise, but for the Purchaser's sole benefit and at the Purchaser's expense (excepting cases of the Owner's breach of warranty or undertaking), to enforce and protect the motion picture rights and all other rights, licenses and privileges herein conveyed under any common law or statutory rights including any and all copyrights and renewals and extensions thereof, and to prevent the infringement thereof, and also to protect the title or titles of the Property, and to litigate, collect and retain all damages arising from any past or future infringement of any or all such rights anywhere and to join the Owner at the Purchaser's sole judgment as a party plaintiff or defendant in any such action. All damages, penalties, settlements and profits relating to or arising from any interference with or infringement of any of the rights, licenses, privileges or property herein granted are hereby assigned to the Purchaser. The Owner agrees to cooperate with the Purchaser in connection with any suit or action threatened or instituted anywhere by or against the Purchaser relating to any rights herein conveyed, or the exercise thereof by the Purchaser, to the full extent of the Owner's ability.

5. The Owner warrants and represents that the Owner is the sole owner of and controls all of the rights, licenses, privileges and property herein conveyed including the unlimited world-wide motion picture and allied rights in the Property and has full and sole right and authority to convey the rights herein

granted including the waiver of *droit moral* made
herein. The Owner further warrants and represents that
the Property is wholly original with the Author in all
respects and that no material therein contained and no
part thereof was taken from or based upon any other
literary or dramatic, graphic or musical material or any
program, publication or motion picture unless explicitly
recited herein and that its full use hereunder will not
in any way infringe upon or violate the copyright or
other rights or licenses of any party whomsoever; that
the Property is or can be validly copyrighted or
registered in the United States of America and likewise
is or can be protected under the Universal Copyright
Convention and Berne Convention and otherwise so far
as the laws of other countries and treaties provide for
such protection; that no part of the Property is in the
public domain or is currently subject to statutory
reversion or termination anywhere; that quality control
and use adequate for protection of any trademarks and
service marks relating to the Property have been
maintained wherever essential; that no part of the
motion picture and allied rights to the Property or any
of the other rights, licenses, privileges or property
herein conveyed has in any way been encumbered,
licensed, conveyed, granted or otherwise disposed of
and that the rights are free and clear of any liens,
financial obligations or claims whatsoever in favor of
any party, including governmental authority, and such
rights and the full right to exercise them have not been
in any way prejudiced, limited, diminished or impaired;
that the title or titles and sub-titles of the Property may
be used legally by the Purchaser in the exercise of all
or any of the rights herein conveyed; that the use,
reproduction, performance or exhibition of the Property, or any part thereof, in the exercise of any of the
rights herein conveyed will not in any way infringe
upon the rights of any party anywhere, or constitute
any libel or other defamation or invasion of the rights
of privacy or publicity; that nothing in the Property
suggests or condones activities that support claims for
product liability, malpractice or consumer deception;
that neither the Owner nor any previous owner of the

Property or any part thereof has done or will do any act or thing that will or may in any way prevent or interfere in any manner with the full and exclusive use by the Purchaser of all of the rights, licenses, privileges and property herein conveyed or which will or may impair or encumber such rights, licenses, privileges or property; that no obligation to employ or engage Author or Owner exists or is hereby created; that there are no claims or litigation pending, outstanding or threatened adversely affecting or that may in any way prejudice the Owner's exclusive rights in the Property, or the copyright or any title thereof or any of the rights, licenses, privileges and property herein conveyed. The Owner warrants and represents that no version or adaptation of or extract from the Property has at any time been recorded, exhibited or performed in any audiovisual medium, phonogram, or radio or authorized for such exhibition or performance except as may be explicitly recited herein, and further represents that all the recitations concerning the Property and its history in ¶2 hereof are accurate, current and complete. The Owner further warrants and represents that if the Owner succeeded to or acts for the successors to the rights granted to the Purchaser herein by will, intestacy or other decedent estate procedure or proceeding anywhere, directly or through intermediaries, the Owner is the sole and lawful executor, heir or other successor to those rights under estate, copyright and other laws of every country and jurisdiction in which an interest in the Property or its proceeds may be asserted, free of adverse claims, tax liens and other encumbrances.

The foregoing warranties and representations are made by the Owner to induce the Purchaser to execute this agreement, and the Owner acknowledges that the Purchaser has executed this agreement in reliance thereon, that the Owner's warranties and indemnities survive any termination of this agreement and that no previous, current or future disclosure by the Owner of any grants, registrations, impediments or other matters shall limit the Owner's warranties or indemnifications. The Owner undertakes to provide that the Owner's immediate successors will be bound by this agreement in the event of the Owner's death or incapacity, or merger. The Owner agrees and guarantees to defend, indemnify and hold the Purchaser and the Purchaser's licensees, assignees, directors, officers, agents and associates, harmless from and against any and all claims, charges, damages, costs, expenses (including reasonable counsel fees), judgments, penalties, liabilities and losses of any other kind or nature whatsoever which may be sustained or suffered by or secured against or imposed upon the Purchaser, or its licensees, assignees, directors, officers, agents or associates by reason of the breach of any of the covenants, representations and warranties herein contained, or by reason of any infringement or violation of any copyright or common law or statutory rights or any literary, dramatic, musical or motion picture or other rights or any right of privacy or any other right of any nature of any party anywhere, or the libel or defamation of any party anywhere, by or on account of any use which the Purchaser may make of the Property or any part thereof including any of its characters and titles, its music, in the making of any motion picture versions, the distribution, exhibition or other disposition of motion picture versions or programs or in the exercise or attempted exercise of any of the other rights, licenses or privileges herein granted.

The warranties, representations and covenants contained in this paragraph apply only to the material used by the Purchaser which is taken from the Property, and do not apply to any extraneous non-derivative matter inserted by the Purchaser.

6. The Owner agrees to ensure that any future publication of the Property, or any derivative or segment thereof, shall bear notice of copyright in such manner and wheresoever required as shall afford it maximum copyright protection. The Purchaser shall be deemed to have acquired and is hereby granted and assigned all rights in the Property under any such copyright which have been herein granted, sold, assigned and set over to the Purchaser, and if

requested by the Purchaser, the Owner agrees at no cost to the Purchaser, to execute, acknowledge and deliver, or cause to be executed, acknowledged and delivered to the Purchaser any instruments that may be required by the Purchaser to establish and vest in the Purchaser such rights under the copyright.

7. The Owner agrees, if applicable and necessary for continued protection, to secure or cause to be secured the renewal of any copyright of the Property at least six (6) months prior to the expiration of any such copyright. In case of any renewal or extension of the United States Copyright or any other copyright in the Property or in any part thereof, under any present or future laws, then the Purchaser shall be deemed to have acquired, and is hereby granted and assigned, under any such renewed copyright, and for the term of any extension thereof, all the rights in the Property which have been herein granted, sold, assigned and set over to the Purchaser and, if requested by the Purchaser, the Owner agrees to execute, acknowledge and deliver, or cause to be duly executed, acknowledged and delivered to the Purchaser any instruments that may be required by the Purchaser or that may be necessary, proper or expedient to establish the vesting in the Purchaser of such rights under the renewal and during such extended period. In the event of the failure of the Owner to do any and all acts necessary to obtain any such renewal within the time hereinabove provided, or to secure any such extension, or to execute or obtain the execution of the instruments above mentioned, the Owner hereby appoints the Purchaser his or its irrevocable attorney-in-fact with the right in the name and on behalf of the Owner (but the Purchaser shall not be obligated), to execute and file all such documents and to do any and all acts and things necessary for the obtaining of any such renewal or extension of copyright.

8. The Purchaser agrees to state or provide that there be stated on positive prints of the film of any motion picture version or on the "crawl" of any

television program based to a substantial extent upon the Property that such motion picture version or program is based on a story, literary or dramatic material written by the Author, or other words to that effect. Further with reference to billing credit but without assuming any obligation to enforce it in its grants to third parties, and subject to circumstances beyond its control and to inadvertent omission, the Purchaser agrees:

---

9. The Owner will not cause, allow or sanction any future publication, novelization or dramatization of the Property, or any part thereof, or any arrangement, translation or revision thereof in any part of the world, or in any form or language, without first granting to, reserving or securing for the Purchaser, without further consideration, all of the rights, licenses and privileges herein conveyed to the Purchaser, and in any grants or agreements hereafter made or entered into by the Owner concerning the Property the Owner will expressly except and reserve the rights herein conveyed to the Purchaser.

The Owner agrees to do or cause to be done all such acts and things as shall be necesary to prevent the Property and any future dramatizations, translations, revisions, novelizations, versions, derivatives or re-issues thereof from falling into the public domain in any country until the expiration of the period of copyright or similar protection therein, as such period may be renewed or extended.

In the event of a novelization, dramatization, translation, adaptation, derivative, revision, character spin-off, rearrangement or new version of the Property, no matter by whom composed, and whether or not written "for hire," the Owner agrees to grant, and does hereby grant to the Purchaser without further consideration the same rights, licenses and privileges therein (supported by equal warranties) which are by the terms hereof conveyed in or made concerning the Property by the Owner to the Purchaser.

10. As total consideration for all of the Owner's grants and undertakings herein, the Purchaser agrees to pay the Owner or the Owner's agent or other representative designated in writing, and with the understanding that all of the payments hereinafter recited encompass and are inclusive of payment to the Owner and to all agents, publishers, collaborators, previous grantors and other third parties having any claim by virtue of arrangements with the Owner, the following compensation less any and all advances previously paid to the Owner for options under this or any other agreement relating to the Property;

(a) On the execution and coming into effect of this agreement by the furnishing of notice of option exercise if applicable, the sum of _____ U.S. DOLLARS (US$ _____) payable in accordance with the following schedule:
If the first production hereunder is a television motion picture, mini-series or special, then any new feature-length photoplay intended for theatrical release and subsequently produced hereunder will be deemed a remake or sequel as the case may be.

(b) The contingent compensation specified in Exhibit 1 annexed hereto and made part hereof by incorporation,* if applicable, and the (further) contingent compensation specified in subparagraphs (c)-(i) below, in each case total, dependent on the happening of the recited event and free of any implied obligation to engender such compensation;

(c) For the first television motion picture or television mini-series based on the Property and produced hereunder, the sum of _____ U.S. DOLLARS (US$ _____) payable on the completion of

---

*Net profits schedule omitted.

principal photography or tape recording, provided however that if the first production hereunder is a television motion picture or television mini-series, then no consideration will be payable under this subparagraph (c) and it will be deemed that the payment specified in subparagraph (a) above for a feature-length photoplay intended for initial theatrical release constitutes full payment under this subparagraph (c).

(d) For each feature length motion picture sequel intended for initial theatrical release based on the Property and produced hereunder, the following:

(i) For the first such sequel the sum of _____ U.S. DOLLARS (US$ _____) payable on completion of principal photography of such sequel;

(ii) For the second such sequel the sum of _____ U.S. DOLLARS (US$ _____) payable on completion of principal photography of such sequel; and

(iii) For the third and all succeeding such sequels, in each case the sum of _____ U.S. DOLLARS (US$ _____) payable on completion of principal photography of such sequel.

(e) For each feature length motion picture remake intended for initial theatrical release and based on the Property and produced hereunder, the sum of _____U.S. DOLLARS (US$ _____) payable on the completion of principal photography of such remake.

(f) For each sequel or remake television motion picture including any sequel or remake mini-series based on the Property and produced hereunder following production of any first television motion picture pursuant to subparagraph (c) above, running two or more hours and neither a series pilot nor episode, the sum of _____U.S. DOLLARS (US$) payable on completion of principal photography of such television motion picture sequel or remake.

(g) For each live or videotape television special based on the Property and produced hereunder the following amount payable within ten (10) days after initial U.S. network television broadcast or release for syndication in major U.S. markets (but not both), whichever is sooner, provided however that if the first production hereunder is a television special, then no consideration will be payable under this subparagraph (g) and it will be deemed that the payment specified in subparagraph (a) above for a feature-length photoplay intended for theatrical release constitutes full payment under this subparagraph (g):

(i) For a special 30–60 minutes inclusive of commercial time, _____ U.S. DOLLARS (US$ _____);

(ii) For a special 60–90 minutes inclusive of commerical time, _____ U.S. DOLLARS (US$ _____); and

(iii) For a special 90 minutes or more inclusive of commercial time, _____ U.S. DOL-LARS (US$ _____).

(h) For each episode in a television series, including any broadcast pilot program, based on the Property and produced hereunder, the following amounts payable within ten (10) days after initial U.S. network television broadcast or release for syndication in major U.S. markets (but not both), whichever is soonest:

(i) For each new series episode less than 15 minutes in length inclusive of commercial time the sum of _____ U.S. DOLLARS (US$ _____);

(ii) For each new series episode between 15–30 minutes in length inclusive of commercial time the sum of _____ U.S. DOLLARS (US$ _____); and

(iii) For each new series episode between 30–60 minutes in length inclusive of commercial time the sum of _____ U.S. DOLLARS (US$ _____).

(i) For any U.S. and Canadian network television reruns of each series episode specified in subparagraph (h) above, residual payments of ONE HUNDRED PERCENT (100%) of the applicable royalty spread equally over five runs so that TWENTY

PERCENT (20%) of such original royalty will be payable each for the second through sixth runs with no further residual compensation due after such sixth run, provided that nothing herein limits the Purchaser's rights to effect unlimited runs throughout the world. For any special(s) within subparagraph (g), the initial royalty therein provided shall prepay two runs of the program over every television station throughout the world and the TWENTY PERCENT (20%) residual payments shall commence with the third such run and be applicable through the seventh, all based on the subparagraph (g) figure notwithstanding that a payment under subparagraph (a) may have been applied. If two or more television motion pictures or programs are combined for theatrical exhibition with or without new material, the resultant version shall not be treated as a sequel and no sequel payment shall become due for its cinematic exhibition. Residual payments where applicable will be made at the time and in the manner prescribed for writers of the screenplay. Contingent compensation for cable and video cassette uses of the Property is not governed by the television provisions in (c)-(i) above, but by Exhibit I.

Except as set forth above and in Exhibit I if applicable, no additional compensation shall be due to the Owner for any other uses or re-uses of the Property in any medium anywhere. If Exhibit I entitles the Owners to a percentage of the Purchaser's share of net profits, nothing in the definition of net profits or in any arrangements for audits by the Owner shall, unless the Purchaser consents, conflict with the applicable provisions in the Purchaser's agreement with its distributor or other financier(s).

11. The Purchaser shall have the continuing right to withhold from the Owner's compensation any taxes required to be withheld by applicable laws and treaties.

12. In the exercise of its reserved rights, the Owner shall have no right to use any of the Purchaser's

motion picture or other "tie-in" material including logo, cover, credits, legends, advertising and still photography and the Owner similarly shall have no rights to use any new literary, musical, graphic or other material which the Purchaser develops, creates or commissions whether or not derivative of the Property.

13. The Owner hereby grants to the Purchaser a right of first refusal in respect of Author-written sequels.

(a) An "Author-written sequel" is defined as any literary work whether written before or after the Property, and whether written by the Author or by a successor in interest of the Author, using one or more characters, titles or other recurring devices appearing in the Property but in a different plot.

(b) A "right of first refusal" is a right to be advised in writing each time the Owner or Author or permitted successor(s) is considering a third party offer for use of Author-written sequels and/or rights reserved by or reverting from third parties to the Owner or Author, as later specified herein, coupled with a right on the Purchaser's part to meet the substantial business terms of each such rival offer by furnishing the Owner with written notice to that effect, If the Purchaser so elects, dispatched within sixty (60) days of the Purchaser's receipt of the written communication outlining rival terms, and to acquire the rights in question by thus signifying the Purchaser's equal offer.

14. All rights of production and use upon the regular legitimate stage with living actors appearing and speaking in person in the actual and immediate presence of the audience, are specifically reserved to the Owner. The Owner agrees not to exercise or authorize exercise of such stage rights for a period of seven (7) years after the date of first general release in the U.S. of any first motion picture hereunder or ten (10) years after the date of the Purchaser's option exercise (if applicable), or ten (10) years from the date of this agreement, whichever date shall latest occur.

Owner's reserved stage rights do not include any right to broadcast, transmit or record any stage performance or any segments thereof.

In any event legitimate stage rights and any other rights in the Property reserved to the Author shall be subject to a right of first refusal in favor of the Purchaser as defined in paragraph 13(b) above except only those print media publication rights that do not come within the definition of Author-written sequels. Similarly subject to a right of first refusal, insofar as consonant with the applicable copyright statute country by country, are whatever rights in the Property may revert to the Author or the Owner from the Purchaser either automatically or by the invocation of termination rights pursuant to statute.

15. Subject to the Purchaser's right of first refusal as to Author-written sequels and to (b) and (c) below and to Purchaser's other rights under this agreement, the Owner reserves the following rights in and to the Property:

(a) Publication and republication rights in the print media;

(b) All rights of production on the legitimate stage with living actors appearing and speaking in person in the actual and immediate presence of an audience, as provided in paragraph 14 above; and

(c) Radio rights, where the script is broadcast direct from living actors.

The Owner agrees to withhold the exercise and/or licensing of its rights reserved under (c) above until the expiration of five (5) years following the first general release in the U.S. of the first motion picture version based in whole or in part on the Property or seven (7) years from the date of this agreement, whichever shall last occur. Any other rights not specifically reserved to the Owner or specifically enumerated among the Owner's grants to the Purchaser shall be deemed included within the Owner's grants to the Purchaser.

16. Nothing in this agreement is designed to limit the Purchaser's right to produce or distribute compet-

itive productions including those based on any Author-written sequels, either in respect of timing or otherwise, or to limit the Purchaser's rights to use public domain material, and insofar as the Property may enter the public domain in a particular country or countries, the Purchaser shall thereafter (without waiving its other rights and remedies hereunder) be relieved of any obligation to make further payment to the Owner for use of the Property in the country or countries where the Property has entered the public domain.

17. The Purchaser shall have the right to assign this agreement fully or in part to anyone anywhere and at any time, provided, however, that the Purchaser shall remain liable for payment of the compensation hereinabove provided if its assignee defaults. The Owner may assign only the Owner's benefits under this agreement. This agreement shall inure to the benefit of the Purchaser's heirs, representatives, successors and assigns forever and shall be binding on the Owner's heirs, representatives, successors and assigns.

18. Nothing herein is designed to create any joint venture, partnership, agency relationship, taxable entity or right of one party to pledge the other's credit.

19. If the Owner is more than one person, all references herein to the Owner shall be deemed references to each and all such persons and all agreements and warranties of the Owner shall be their joint and several agreements and warranties.

20. The Owner agrees to execute at the Purchaser's request and deliver to the Purchaser any additional documents or instruments which the Purchaser may reasonably require to give effect to the intent of this agreement and convey to the Purchaser good and marketable rights in and to the Property. Without limiting the generality of the foregoing, the Owner agrees concurrently herewith to furnish and to cause any publisher or other third party claiming any interest in the Property to furnish in form reasonably satisfac-

tory to the Purchaser a short form consent, quitclaim or assignment suitable for recording and registration at the Purchaser's election. The Owner irrevocably appoints the Purchaser its attorney-in-fact with the full power to execute such instruments in the Owner's name and stead should the Owner fail timely to comply with the provisions of this paragraph, and the Owner acknowledges that the authority given the Purchaser is a power coupled with an interest.

21. All notices furnished under this agreement shall be addressed as follows:
To the Purchaser: _____
_____
_____
To the Owner: _____
_____
_____

or at such other address as the respective party may from time to time designate by written notice to the other, and shall be served by mail (postage prepaid), telegraph or cable (charges prepaid), so addressed or by personal delivery. The date of mailing or delivery to the telegraph office or of personal delivery as the case may be shall be deemed to be the date of service.

22. This agreement including the exhibit(s) annexed hereto fully sets out the agreement between the parties concerning the Property, superseding all other agreements between them, and may not be altered except by written instrument executed by both parties hereto. This agreement shall be governed by, subject to and interpreted in accordance with the laws of the State of _____.

IN WITNESS WHEREOF, the undersigned have executed this agreement the day and year first above written.

Owner: Purchaser:

_____   _____

PUBLISHER'S QUITCLAIM

Dear Sirs:

We understand that you are about to obtain from
_____ (hereinafter referred to as the
"Author") the motion picture and other rights in and to
a literary work entitled _____ , published
or to be published by us. This letter confirms that you
may make an agreement to that effect with the Author
or the Author's designee without consulting us and
that you may exercise your rights under that agreement
free of any claim or interference by us.

We acknowledge that the publication of excerpts,
summaries and novelizations from or based on the
above work or on your motion picture(s) or television
programs, not exceeding 10,000 words in length, is not
a violation of our rights and we waive any objection
thereto.

Very truly yours,

Comments

This form is unlike its predecessor in that it reflects no effort
to be diplomatic. Quite the contrary, it tries saying it all, and
insofar as it falls short of doing so, you can be sure that the miss
is unintentional. Things could scarcely be otherwise when you
consider the cost of a major film or television project nowadays.

Even so, this American form that looks prototypical at first
glance has its odd features. The more traditional elements are
present, an extendable option, a long recitation of rights granted
and a shorter one of rights withheld, the book publisher's not
always essential consent to limited publication and reference to
the short form "Assignment" that can be recorded in the U.S.
Copyright Office without disclosing the whole arrangement to
those put on notice of the rights transfer. The following provisions, however, deserve comment:

1) First and foremost, the Property is better defined than in
   most film contracts, with Paragraph 2 adhering to our
   tenets.

2) Subparagraphs (g) and (h) of 3 pick up "initially or at any time" to avoid claims of improper sequence, and "component elements" of the Property are made available in (k) for use as a lead-in to exploitation of trademarks as in (l) and 4.

3) The warranties in Paragraph 5 recite that the trademarks have been maintained with proper quality control, a point not always seen in company with the more traditional assurances.

4) Paragraph 9 goes pretty far in granting parallel rights to future derivatives, no matter who writes them.

5) Some tough first refusals in Paragraphs 13 and 14 protect the buyer at least in some degree against losing future harvests.

These are all themes familiar from Part I of this handbook. Perhaps the most noteworthy provisions here are definitions of the Property. A more vivid and extreme effort to that end will be set out in Form C, but harbingers of things to come appear in what next follows.

Form C:
A Character
Definition

FORM C: A CHARACTER DEFINITION

1. INDIVIDUAL NAME(S):
2. GROUP NAME(S):
3. NAME VARIANTS IN DIFFERENT LANGUAGES:
4. SOBRIQUETS (NICKNAMES):
5. SLOGAN PHRASES USED TO IDENTIFY CHARACTERS BY THEMSELVES OR BY OTHERS:
6. MAIN HABITAT IF ON PREEXISTING EARTHLY OR STELLAR MAPS:
7. MAIN FICTITIOUS HABITAT WITH DESCRIPTION AND IMAGINARY MAP IF ANY ANNEXED: (Mark with reference to this Number 7.)
8. ERA(S) INCLUDING ANY TIME PERIOD OR EVENT FRAMEWORK OF SIGNIFICANCE:
9. CHARACTERISTIC DRAWINGS AND OTHER GRAPHIC DEPICTIONS ANNEXED: (Mark with reference to this Number 9.)
10. BRIEF PHYSICAL DESCRIPTION:
11. MAIN OCCUPATION:
12. CHARACTERISTIC MODE OF SPEECH AND KEY PHRASES:
13. ORIGINAL LANGUAGE:
14. FICTITIOUS ADDRESS:

15. RECURRING TRAITS AND OTHER CHARACTERIS-
    TICS:
16. PROPS INCLUDING RECURRING COSTUMES, MAS-
    COTS, AND OTHER PHYSICAL DEVICES, WITH
    NAMES IF ANY:
17. IDENTIFYING THEME MUSIC IF ANY: (Specify title
    and mention any U.S. Copyright Registration,
    recordings, broadcasts, and other transmissions
    worldwide.)
18. FICTITIOUS ORGANIZATION TO WHICH CHARAC-
    TER(S) BELONG(S) WITH RANK OR TITLE:
19. NAME AND SUMMARY OF FICTITIOUS CAUSE OR
    PHILOSOPHY IDENTIFIED WITH CHARACTER(S):
20. CONTINUING PROJECT OR MISSION:
21. FOILS AND OTHER ANCILLARY CHARACTERS
    INCLUDED IN THE GRANT OF RIGHTS SUBJECT
    TO CONTRACT PROVISIONS ON "SPIN-OFF": (In
    some cases, these are best listed on separate
    forms. Where not separately listed, a brief summary
    of their recurring elements according with the form
    will be useful.)
22. USES OF CHARACTER NAME(S) AS BOOK, PRO-
    DUCTION, AND GAME TITLES:
23. NAME OF FIRST BOOK AND/OR PUBLICLY PER-
    FORMED VEHICLE IN WHICH CHARACTER(S)
    FIRST APPEARED ANYWHERE:
24. FIRST PUBLICATION DATE OF 23 ABOVE:
25. COPYRIGHT NOTICE WORDING AND PLACEMENT
    WITH 24 ABOVE:
26. FIRST UNITED STATES PUBLICATION DATE OF 23
    ABOVE:
27. FIRST UNITED STATES COPYRIGHT NOTICE
    WORDING AND PLACEMENT WITH 23 ABOVE:
28. U.S. COPYRIGHT OFFICE ORIGINAL AND RE-
    NEWAL REGISTRATIONS CONCERNING PRODUC-
    TIONS IN ALL MEDIA WHERE THE CHARACTER(S)
    APPEAR(S):
29. LIST ASSIGNMENTS AND OTHER RELEVANT DOC-
    UMENTS RECORDED ANYWHERE:
30. DATE OF FIRST U.S. TRADEMARK USE OF
    CHARACTER WITH IDENTIFICATION OF LICENSEE
    OR OTHER USER:

31. EXTRACT OF QUALITY CONTROL PROVISIONS IN PREVIOUSLY GRANTED LICENSES OF THE CHARACTER(S):
32. TRADEMARK CAPTIONING OF THE CHARACTER(S) AND/OR PROPS TO DATE:
33. REGISTRATION OF THE CHARACTER(S) AND/OR PROPS WORLDWIDE,SPECIFYING DATE, NUMBER, AND CLASSIFICATION:
34. WORKS IN WHICH CHARACTER(S) APPEAR(S):
35. ORIGINAL LITERARY AUTHOR(S) OF EACH WORK LISTED IN 34 ABOVE:
36. ORIGINAL GRAPHIC CREATOR(S) OF EACH WORK LISTED IN 34 ABOVE:
37. DATE OF DEATH OF ANY IN 35 AND/OR 36 ABOVE:
38. TRANSLATIONS, NEW DRAWINGS, AND OTHER EMBELLISHMENTS ALTERING THE CHARACTER(S) AFTER ORIGINAL DEPICTION:
39. AUTHORS AND ILLUSTRATORS, DATES AND CIRCUMSTANCES OF ALTERATIONS IN 38 ABOVE:
40. APPROXIMATE SIZE OF CHARACTER(S')'S AUDIENCE WORLDWIDE TO DATE VIA USE IN ALL MEDIA, INCLUDING COMMERCIALS AND MERCHANDISING:
41. CURRENTLY OUTSTANDING LICENSEE OPTIONS OR OTHER CIRCUMSTANCES INDICATING FUTURE CONTINUED USE OF CHARACTER(S):
42. PROPOSED CHARACTER ALTERATIONS AND NEW ANCILLARY CHARACTERS UNDER CONSIDERATION WITH AUTHORITY OF RIGHTS OWNER:
43. ANY PERTINENT QUOTES FROM REVIEWS OR PRIZE AWARDS (Annex if lengthy):
44. IDENTIFICATION ANYWHERE AS COMMERCIAL SPOKESPERSON(S) FOR PRODUCT OR SERVICE:
45. ORIGINAL MODE OF PRESENTATION IN DRAMATIC FORM, *E.G.,* LIVE ACTORS, ANIMATION, PUPPETS:
46. SUBSEQUENT MODES OF PRESENTATION IN DRAMATIC FORM, INCLUDING THEME PARKS, PAGEANTS:
47. IDENTIFICATION WITH ANY "LIVE" PERFORMER, LIVING OR DECEASED, INCLUDING VOICE ONLY:

48. NAME OF ANY REAL CHARACTER(S) ON WHOM BASED:
49. NAMES AND ADDRESSES OF OWNERS AND LICENSING AGENTS: (Questions of estate succession, previous licensees and other matters are left out because these and some of the points in this form belong properly in contract warranties.)
50. MISCELLANEOUS POINTS AS FURTHER DESCRIPTION:

Comments

Fictional characters, really a new form of property, are so hard to define that nobody tries to in drafting contracts. One finds the name and perhaps even a picture or two, but nothing in great depth. People in real life defy thumbnail summary, and so it is unremarkable that people in books and shows are just as elusive. The analogy breaks down, however, when fictional characters become licensed assets. Here the rules change, and definition becomes plausible.

Form C is arranged in a definition format and set up like a questionnaire. Unlike other examples cited here it has not found its way into actual usage, and seems unlikely to do so. It was published originally in the periodical *Communications and the Law* and has been taken up at least once in Holland, but otherwise it seems pure theory. Whether it need remain so, only time will show. If nothing else, it suggests a check list for transactions concerning prime industrial assets. Someday, perhaps, fictional characters may be defined in exhibits annexed to main agreements.

Our suggested form is nearly self-explanatory. Only two points need mention:

1) The form addresses its characters' history, not only their dimensions

2) Trademark as well as copyright elements attract the attention they deserve.

It may be interesting (if not always profitable) exposing the year's top multi-million-dollar characters to the proposed test. If none come to mind, we can always begin with Mr. Sherlock Holmes and his associate Watson.

Form D:
Merchandising
Agency

FORM D: MERCHANDISING AGENCY

DUTCHCO B.V. c/o SCRIBBLERS, LTD. ("Licensor") and LONDON GROUP ("Licensee") agree as follows this ___ day of _____, 19 ___ .

1) The following definitions apply:

The Property is that series of literary works by Fielding Smollett known cumulatively as "The Adventures of Tom Random" and by individual titles listed below, it being understood however that the Property and the grant of rights in this agreement are confined to the original Smollett writings in the listed novels but do not include (and Licensee will indemnify Licensor for using or sub-licensing) any literary, graphic, or other material ever created or furnished in any context by the BBC, CBS, Raoul Gomez or any other contributor of derivative elements;

Merchandising Rights are the non-transferable and non-exclusive right to design and produce, or to license others to design and produce in the latter instance under contracts whose terms and forms are subject to Licensor's advance written approval, merchandise items derivative of the Property such as maps, clothing, posters, chinaware, games and figurines;

The Territory is the entire world except the USA, its

territories, possessions, commonwealths and dependencies, Canada and Japan;

The Term is a period of two (2) years from the date of this agreement, subject to foreshortening as provided below, or for Licensee's breach, whichever sooner occurs.

2) Licensor hereby grants Merchandising Rights to Licensee for the Territory and Term, reserving to itself (as between the parties and on behalf of the underlying owner Shonan Pte. Ltd.) all copyright, trademark, exploitation and other rights not explicitly granted, and with the understanding that Licensee will never, during or after the Term, oppose or challenge Licensor's or Licensor's designee's absolute ownership and title including rights that subsequently revert to Licensor and that any and all goodwill, derivative material and other intangible assets arising anywhere in the course of Licensee's exercise of its Merchandising Rights will from the moment of creation belong to and inure solely for the benefit of Licensor's designee, and the Property's owner, Shonan Pte. Ltd.

3) Licensee undertakes to use best endeavours toward the turning to account of the rights this agreement appoints it to administer and agrees, notwithstanding Licensor's right of advance written approval over sublicensing agreements, to ensure that all its grantees will implement by further documentation (if required) Shonan Pte. Ltd.'s ownership provided for in ¶2 above and will itself furnish implementing documentation promptly at Licensor's request, hereby appointing Licensor irrevocably its attorney in fact to do so in Licensee's name and stead in the event of Licensee's refusal or delay.

4) Within as well as outside the Territory Licensor and/or Shonan Pte. Ltd. shall at all times have the sole right but not obligation to initiate, conduct, compromise and settle litigation and opposition proceedings concerning the Property (deducting up to ___ % of Licensee's commission for Licensor's legal cost if Licensee declines to participate in litigation against

infringers and/or delinquent accounts) and to effect trademark, copyright and other registrations in the name of Licensor or its designee, in each instance with Licensee's full cooperation.

5) Each party warrants and represents to the other and will indemnify the other for breach of its own warranty, its freedom lawfully to make this agreement, and that whatever literary and other material it furnishes in connection with Merchandising Rights, e.g. visual derivatives commissioned by Licensee, will notwithstanding Licensor's approval of product and arrangements be devoid of infringing, libelous and other unlawful matter and of residual payment, billing credit, moral right restrictions and other obligations to third parties except as Licensor may advise.

6) Nothing in this agreement, which Licensor but not Licensee may assign at any time, is intended to limit in any way Licensor's reserved rights whether or not competitive with Licensee in the Territory, or to extend by implication Licensee's rights or percentage sharing, as hereinafter provided, either in respect of time or product or media, or to make derivatives or spin-offs of products licensed hereunder commissionable.

7) Licensee makes an additional special warranty and representation, in which its principal Samuel T. Coleridge joins by his individual signature below, that their arrangements with the BBC, and their earlier merchandising of the Property in BBC's behalf, in no way conflict with, impede or adversely affect its or his ability to make and perform this agreement, or Licensor's undisturbed realization of anticipated benefits and rights arising from its performance.

8) As its total compensation, which is inclusive of any payments divisible by internal arrangement with or owing to the BBC, Mr. Coleridge and all others, Licensee shall be entitled to retain agency commissions in the form of sums equal to Thirty Per Cent (30%) of net royalties actually received by or for Licensor under Licensor-approved contracts for the

disposition of Merchandising rights where Licensee was the original and effective cause of introducing a third party sublicensee in the Territory and during the Term.

9) Such Licensee commissions, once payable, survive as obligations for a period of ___ years after expiry of the Term in due course (but not for Licensee's breach) with pro rating of receipts where the sublicense accounting period is unsynchronized with this post-Term Licensee entitlement period at the completion of which all Licensee entitlements automatically terminate, but in Licensor-approved instances where Licensee itself manufactures the product, Licensor's royalties, quality control provisions and other terms such as Licensee's sell-off rights will be agreed case by case and contracted separately.

10) Licensee will furnish Licensor with copies of all proposed and final sublicensing agreements concerning the Property for approval, as well as quarterly accountings subject to Licensor's continuing post-Term audit and inspection rights to review and copy relevant portions of Licensee's books and records, but Licensee shall remit collections immediately to Licensor (after deducting its stipulated commission) rather than holding it to accompany the quarterly statement.

11) Licensor requirements for copyright, trademark and other captioning and for advertisements and announcements concerning the Property will be furnished to and adhered to by Licensee and its sub-licensees from time to time.

12) This document sets out the full agreement between the parties, is governed by the laws of England and may not be altered except in writing signed by Licensor and Licensee.

Dutchco B.V.

By: _____

London Group

By: _____

I join in London Group's
warranties and representations as
a material inducement to secure
Licensor's signature.

_____

S. T. Coleridge

List of individual titles:

_____

_____

_____

Comments

In this form the agent is appointed in terms designed to ensure ownership of all intellectual property by the non-signatory owner. That concept was developed in earlier text, and here we see it in the third party provisions of Paragraphs 2 and 3. Other features worth noting are as follows:

1) The rights are non-exclusive, and Paragraph 8 actually requires the agent to have initiated the transaction as a condition of beind paid.

2) Several of the provisions such as 7 reflect previous limited grants to the BBC, and the narrow definition of the Property further confines the agent to material in the original books.

3) Paragraph 9 contemplates actual product manufacture by the regional agent, leaving the terms unsettled to the Dutch licensor's advantage since its consent will eventually be required.

4) In Paragraph 10 the agent remits immediately on collection before quarterly accountings.

These features, together with the grudging Term and Territory, combine in a pattern too harsh for any agent to accept without amendment. The main thing, however, is how the absent owner is brought into it for the benefits without the burdens. That, at least, is the philosophy. Whether it works will depend largely on the agent's contracts with sublicensees, not shown here.

Those in turn must reflect the above terms, and will be subject to approval.

Form E:
A Television Option
Agreement

FORM E: A TELEVISION OPTION AGREEMENT

TELEVISION OPTION AGREEMENT

Beaumaris Productions Limited of Mona, North Wales ("the Company") and Lenox Uppereastside Hill of New York City ("Author") agree as follows this ___ day of _____ 19 ___ concerning the Author's book entitled STALIN REMEMBERED published by Pinko Press, Inc. on or about the ___ day of September 19 ___ (the "Property"):

1) For consideration of Five Thousand Dollars ($U.S. 5000) constituting a non-returnable advance against the amount specified in clause (3) below, Author grants to the Company the exclusive option, to be exercised if the Company elects to proceed, by furnishing Author with written notice to that effect within a period of one year from the date above written accompanied by requisite payment, to acquire all television dramatization, broadcasting, cable, satellite, closed circuit, non-theatric and videogram world-wide rights to the Property for a special, mini-series or made-for-television film in connection with which the Author shall have rights of prior consultation in respect of his own depiction and other creative matters.

2) The Company's option may be extended for an additional one year period upon written notice furnished the Author within the original option period accompanied by a further non-returnable advance in the sum of Three Thousand Five Hundred Dollars (U.S. $3,500).

3) Upon exercise of the option the Company shall pay to the Author the further non-returnable sum of Seventy-Five Thousand Dollars (U.S. $75,000) less the advance(s) paid for the option and its extension (if applicable).

4) (a) In addition, the Author shall be entitled to receive (with quarterly statements, copies of all sublicensing agreements and audit rights exercisable at reasonable business hours) sums equal to two and one-half percent (2½%) of one hundred percent (100%) of net profits derived from any and all sources and media everywhere engendered by the Company's direct or indirect exploitation of its rights hereunder. Net profits are all sums remaining after deduction of reasonable production and distribution expenses (excluding overheads) consonant with industry practise and not cross-collateralized with any other production. The Company, in turn, provided it shall have effectively exercised its option, shall be entitled to Five Per Cent (5%) of any increase in Author's net royalties from the Property in book form in territories where national telecast of a programme based on the Property as reissued in a new edition timed to coincide with such telecast shall have occurred. Such increase, if any, shall be computed over a course of one year and accounted in a manner parallel to the Company's accounting above.

(b) Author shall be entitled to ___ free copies of the videogram(s) in every form and language utilized for his private use only and not for commercial gain.

(c) Commencing with the commissioning of a teleplay, outline or treatment, or other pre-production activity (whichever is earliest) the Company will pay to the Author an agreed consultancy fee for non-exclusive services reflecting his expertise in respect of the subject matter.

All of the foregoing provisions for compensation, firm or contingent, are cumulative and conversion into dollars will be made at the most favourable rate to Author occurring during the option period as the same may be extended. In the event of U.K. exchange control reimposition or currency export limitation, the sterling equivalents of payments to Author will be segregated and held in trust for Author in an interest-bearing account for his benefit.

5) All rights not explicitly granted are reserved by Author without limitation of any nature, and upon failure or refusal of the Company to make timely exercise of its applicable option all rights of every nature shall automatically revert to Author without encumbrance. However upon exercise of its option and payment of the full purchase price, the Company's rights shall vest permanently subject only to its best endeavours to effect UK and/or USA national telecast of a programme based on the Property and to Author's right, upon notice, to repurchase the rights (if Author so elects) at the original purchase price plus prime interest if no such telecast has occurred within five (5) years from the date on which the Company exercised its option.

6) In any production based on the Property and in all paid advertising and promotion thereof issued by or under the control of the Company, subject to third-party failure to credit him in publicity, Author shall be accorded billing credit on a single video frame in type of size not less than fifty percent (50%) the size of type used for the title, as follows:

From the book *STALIN REMEMBERED* By L.U. Hill
Story Consultant, L.U. Hill

7) As a sole and limited exception to his reservation of ancillary and all other rights not explicitly granted, Author consents on a quitclaim basis, and subject to working out provisions for quality control

and additional royalties, to the Company's acquisition
of such merchandising tie-up rights as may derive from
the Property itself as distinct from its underlying
subject matter, with the understanding that any and all
essential merchandising clearances and waivers will be
the Company's responsibility to secure from third
parties.

8) Author warrants and represents that the Property is original except for quoted or public domain
sources and is free of libel, infringing and other
unlawful material, and that he is free lawfully to make
this agreement. The Company warrants and represents
that it is free to make this agreement and that its
adaptation(s) of the Property including all new material,
notwithstanding consultation with Author, will be
original and free of libel, infringing and other unlawful
material. Each party will be responsible for its own
material including without limitation alterations of the
Property as published and departures from satisfactory
releases. Each of the parties will indemnify the other
for breach of its respective warranties. The Company
agrees that it will not depict or refer to any person who
has not signed a release satisfactory to Author and the
Company, a list of which has been furnished by
Author. The Company has also examined the releases
satisfactory to Author.

9) As between the parties, the Company shall be
solely responsible for securing clearances essential to
its own adaptation and for production costs and
overages of every nature. Nothing herein is designed to
create any joint venture, agency, partnership, taxable
entity or right to pledge the other's credit.

10) The Company will at no cost to Author obtain
and disclose to Author an errors and omissions
broadcasters liability insurance policy covering Author
in an amount consonant with industry practise.

11) This sets out the full agreement between the
parties, which cannot be altered except in writing

signed by both parties, and which is governed by the law of England.

Comments

This Anglo-American television sale is included here mainly to illustrate another of our main points, the necessity of releases equal in scope to the proposed mission. Otherwise the form is reasonably straightforward, but the following provisions deserve brief comment:

1) The British company's reward in Paragraph 4(a) for increasing book royalties is scarcely run of the mill.

2) The author's right of consultation concerning his own depiction reflects the biographical nature of this material. Paragraph 1 affords at least a little protection.

3) The author does somewhat better in Paragraph 5, which gives him a repurchase right (obviously with a successor's money) if the Welsh producers get nowhere.

4) In Paragraph 7 we encounter a classic dilemma, separation of basic subject matter from material now in a derivative version. As a practical matter this often conduces impasse resolved by further negotiation. Without more detailed partitioning after adaptation, each side may be unwilling to risk development of its questionable rights.

5) Returning to the main point, a publisher may have secured releases adequate to its limited project but the author needs more for television. Accordingly this contract requires that only signatories to forms drawn up by the author's lawyer will be depicted in the production. Paragraph 8 can be read against release forms suggested earlier.

Form F:
A Rights Investment Portfolio

FORM F: A RIGHTS INVESTMENT PORTFOLIO

RIGHTS DEVELOPMENT FUND, INC.
OPTION AGREEMENT

Date _____

TO: Owner

Dear _____ :

For total consideration in the sum of _____ receipt of which you hereby acknowledge, you hereby grant to us, our assignees and licensees, the irrevocable and exclusive option, to be exercised if we so elect by furnishing you with written notice to that effect at the above address issued on or before the close of business on _____ , 19 ___ , to enter into the annexed purchase agreement with you as "Owner" and us as "Purchaser" and thereby to acquire the percentage share of Proceeds and other rights therein specified. Our option may be extended by an additional period to and including the close of business   on 19 ___ , upon similar written notice to that effect issued at any time before expiry of the original option period accompanied by additional payment in the sum of _____ .

If we elect to and do make timely exercise of our option, all payments theretofore made to you will be deemed advances against the payment specified in paragraph 2 of the annexed purchase agreement.

During the option period(s), all your warranties and representations in the said purchase agreement shall be and remain effective at once commencing on the date of this option agreement, except to any extent that Exhibits recited in the purchase agreement as annexed are missing or incomplete, and you will immediately furnish us with all records and information that will eventually constitute those Exhibits or that relate to your warranties and representations incorporated by reference herein.

You further warrant and represent that your next Accounting from Distributor (both as defined in the purchase agreement) is contractually due on or before _____ , 19 ___ ; that immediately upon its receipt you will furnish us with an accurate and complete copy; and you agree that during the entirety of the option period(s) you will neither do nor permit anything to be done that might be reasonably anticipated to diminish Proceeds or impair the Property, as defined and proscribed in the purchase agreement. During the option period(s) and thereafter if the option is exercised, we may independently approach Distributor(s) and others for information concerning Proceeds and make derivative works of any nature based on the Property.

If any Accounting or other relevant document or payment is contractually due at any time during the option period(s), and is delayed, the applicable time limit for our exercise of the option will be extended by the period during which its arrival is delayed beyond the due date, plus an additional thirty (30) days.

Nothing herein obligates us to exercise any option or undertake any commitment beyond payment of the advance recited above. If we elect to and do make timely exercise of our option, we will as a condition of its efficacy accompany our notice of option exercise with payment of the amount recited in paragraph 2 of the purchase agreement less advances, together with a fully executed copy of that agreement.

Agreed to: Very truly yours,

_____   _____

PURCHASE AGREEMENT

AGREEMENT made this _____ day of _____, 19 ____, by and between _____ ("Purchaser") whose address is _____ and ("Owner") whose address is _____.

1. For the purposes of this agreement the following definitions shall be applicable:

a. "The Property" refers to the following work(s) or composition(s) by _____, and all derivatives and extricable component elements of the Property including without limitations its title, characters, plots, dialogue, format, adaptations, versions, translations, revisions and other devices and forms not in the public domain:

b. "Source Contracts" means all existing and future agreements and commitments for or relating to the licensing or other uses or exploitation of the Property anywhere in the world, in any form or language, whether or not subsequently enlarged by reversion of any rights from third parties, and in any medium now known or hereafter devised including without limitation "free" network, regional and local television, community antenna and cable television, pay and subscription television, satellite television, closed circuit television, video and audio cassette and cartridges, radio, motion pictures, book publishing and other print media and substitutions for print media, the legitimate theatre and other live performance, merchandising, industrial productions, phonograph records and computers; and without limiting this definition, the parties include more specifically the following agreement(s) annexed hereto in copy form and made part hereof by reference as Exhibit I (A -):

c. "Derivative Contracts" mean any and all existing and future agreements and commitments which are substitutions for or modifications or extensions of Source Contracts, notwithstanding novation or the introduction of Owner's heirs, reversionary estate or other additional parties, and any and all future agreements and commitments with anyone, flowing as an ancillary or subsidiary right from or in connection with a Source Contract, including without limitation "spin-off" agreements providing for new uses of elements composing the Property such as sequels or series in any medium utilizing at least one of the same fictional characters in new settings, or new texts or performing participants presented in substantially the same format, regardless in every case of any change in name, title or subtitle.

d. "Proceeds" include the gross of all royalties and advances against royalties, fees, salaries, stock shares, loans, participations in gross or net profits howsoever defined, shares of box office receipts, prize monies, claims, insurance recoveries and other things of value ever received anywhere by or for Owner, directly or indirectly or through any existing or future entity including any corporation, partnership and trust, and in any capacity including as author, production consultant, director, editor, assignor, licensor, broker or agent, commentator or commercial endorser, whether actually or constructively received or receivable by or held in trust for Owner or any of Owner's existing or future assignees, licensees, heirs, successors, estate, beneficiaries or other designees, from, arising out of, attributable to or connected with any and every Source Contract and Derivative Contract and reversion by operation of law regardless of when the proceeds are created or received as defined above, and with no deductions for agency or managerial commissions, income taxes or other obligations except local taxes and other legally required payments. Proceeds also include tax rebates if and to the extent connected with the Property.

e. "Distributor" means every person, firm, corporation and other entity engaged as licensee or otherwise in the turning to account or effecting the use of the Property in any medium anywhere in connection with a Source Contract or Derivative Contract, and the term includes without limitation any such motion picture, television, phonograph or merchandising distributor as well as any literary or music publisher and any production group whose function, at least in substantial part, comes within the definition in this subparagraph.

f. "Accountings" refers to all written and other statements, whether or not certified, ever disclosing or relating to Proceeds and arrangements concerning Proceeds from Source Contracts and Derivative Contracts, whether issued by Distributor or assignees, licensees, subdistributors, agents, accountants or associates of Distributor, or by any other party including Owner and Owner's heirs and designees, and more particularly, but without narrowing this definition, the royalty or profit statements, or both, annexed hereto in copy form and made part hereof by incorporation as Exhibit II (A -).

g. "Registrations" mean any and all certificates and other records evidencing copyright, trademark, service mark, assignment or other incorporeal rights relating to the Property ever issued, renewed or maintained by governmental, writers' union or other authority anywhere, whether or not connected with any Source Contract or Derivative Contract, and more particularly, but without narrowing this definition, the certificates and supporting data annexed hereto in copy form and made part hereby by incorporation as Exhibit III (A -).

2. For total consideration in the sum of $ _____ receipt of which Owner hereby acknowledges, Owner hereby sells, assigns, transfers, and sets over to Purchaser irrevocably and perpetually, an amount equal to _____ percent (___%) of Owner's share of Proceeds, constituting _____ percent (___%) of One Hundred percent (100%) of Proceeds, from the Source Contracts reproduced as Exhibits I and from all Derivative Contracts relating to the Property, effective in each case (notwithstanding inclusion of any previously contested or delayed payment) commencing the next forthcoming Accounting or payment of Proceeds not accompanied by an Accounting, whichever is sooner, and enduring for as long as there are any Proceeds. This grant is binding upon Owner's

heirs, successors and beneficiaries of any reversionary interest ever relating to the Property insofar as consonant with local laws everywhere, and may be recorded by Purchaser under the laws of any jurisdiction permitting its recordal.

3. Supplementing this grant, and without limiting Purchaser's other rights hereunder, Owner further agrees:

a. That Owner will immediately notify in writing every Distributor and other party responsible for payment of Proceeds under Source Contracts and will promptly, whenever Derivative Contracts are made, notify in writing those similarly responsible for payment of Proceeds under Derivative Contracts, with copies of such notifications to Purchaser, that this present agreement has been entered into and that henceforth Purchaser is to receive separate payment of Purchaser's agreed share of Proceeds together with separate copies of Accountings;

b. That at no cost to Purchaser, Owner will assert whatever legal claims and undertake whatever legal action is necessary anywhere to protect, enlarge and receive Proceeds in accordance with the terms of Source Contracts and Derivative Contracts, hereby appointing Purchaser to act as Owner's attorney-in-fact to do so in Owner's stead in the event of Owner's default, whether as to past or future claims, but without effecting any waiver by Purchaser of Purchaser's rights or remedies for such default against Owner or of Purchaser's rights to assert claims against Owner or of Purchaser's rights to assert claims against third parties anywhere through counsel of Purchaser's own choosing;

c. Similarly at no cost to Purchaser that Owner will secure, maintain, protect, register, record, renew whenever required for extended protection and enforce against third party infringement and dilution all incorporeal rights in the Property, whether or not registered, to the maximum extent permitted by the various domestic and international laws that may be applicable including without limitation the then current

United States Copyright and Trademark Laws and the Universal Copyright Convention, hereby appointing Purchaser to act as attorney-in-fact to do so in Owner's stead in the event of Owner's default, but without effecting any waiver by Purchaser of Purchaser's rights or remedies for such default against Owner or of Purchaser's right to assert claims against third parties anywhere through counsel of Purchaser's own choosing;

      d. That to the maximum extent permitted under Source Contracts and Derivative Contracts, and by explicit provision in any new Derivative Contracts, Owner will arrange that Purchaser be in a position to inherit and assert Owner's other rights against Distributor(s) and other third parties, including without limitation the right to inspect Distributor's books and records, to receive copies of reviews, to take over production and to rescind for want of best efforts to exploit the Property.

      4. Owner's rights set forth in paragraph 3 and elsewhere in this agreement are not designed to create obligations, and Owner may waive or forego the exercise of any such rights one or more times without being deemed to have waived the right to exercise similar or dissimilar rights on any other occasion.

      5. At no time shall Owner assign, encumber, terminate, alter or waive any of Owner's rights under or be in breach of any Source Contract or Derivative Contract, or other source of Proceeds, or enter into any new Derivative Contract without Purchaser's advance written approval, not to be unreasonably withheld, or make any agreement whatsoever concerning the Property that might reasonably be anticipated to impair its value or diminish Proceeds, as by granting competitive licenses in different media or agreeing to price discounts, remaindering or cross-collateralization with earnings and losses from other transactions.

      6. Owner has advised Purchaser that Owner's agent or manager representing the Property is_____,

and a copy of Owner's agreement with the named agent or manager is annexed hereto and made part hereof by reference as Exhibit IV with the understanding that Owner will not waive any of Owner's rights under or consent to alter such agreement without Purchaser's advance written approval, not to be unreasonably withheld. Owner will advise such agent or manager of Owner's obligations to Purchaser and secure cooperation in carrying out its terms.

7. Owner grants to Purchaser the right to use Owner's name, likeness and biographical data concerning Owner, and to disclose, publish and publicize the present agreement fully or in part, whether by itself or in connection with other transactions with others, for any lawful purpose whatsoever including without limitation the assignment of Purchaser's rights hereunder and the securing of investment by third parties in the Property and other properties.

8. If Distributor's rights terminate as the result of abandonment, rescission, reversion or under any other circumstances, Owner will use best efforts to secure additional Source Contracts as a replacement, and the terms will be subject to Purchaser's advance written approval not to be unreasonably withheld. Owner's percentage sharing and other rights herein will immediately become applicable with respect to any such replacement Source Contract(s) and Derivative Contract(s).

9. Owner will write or consent to all further editions, remakes, musical and other adaptations, serializations and other versions of the Property for which a third party offer is made whose acceptance would enhance the possibility of augmenting Proceeds, notwithstanding that alteration or development of the Property may be artistically at variance with Owner's preference. Agreements concerning the resultant versions will be considered Source Contracts or Derivative Contracts that engender Proceeds.

10. Purchaser shall have the right at any time and from time to time to assign, sell, pledge, mortgage, and otherwise encumber and deal with in any way Purchaser's rights and shares hereunder, fully or in part, and Purchaser reserves the right to engage in similar and dissimilar transactions with others at any time anywhere, as investor, producer or in any other capacity, whether or not another property is competitive, and without any fiduciary or implied contractual duty to Owner.

11. At no cost to Purchaser, Owner will cause Purchaser to be included in any and all "errors and omissions" and other insurance coverage relating to the Property, forwarding documentation to that effect to Purchaser promptly after the effective date of this agreement.

12. As security for Owner's performance of all obligations hereunder Owner hereby sells, assigns, transfers and sets over to Purchaser all of Owner's rights in and to the Property including without limitation the benefit of the copyright and all subsidiary rights and Registrations in and to the degree such rights are controlled by Owner, as a security interest recordable by Purchaser at its option in any and all jurisdictions permitting recordal of such interests, and Owner agrees to furnish written notification to all third parties dealing with the Property of Purchaser's interest therein, and to execute on request by Purchaser any instruments including without limitation mortgages and assignments required to give effect to the foregoing, hereby appointing Purchaser to be Owner's attorney-in-fact to do so in Owner's stead in the event of Owner's refusal within a reasonable time upon request.

13. Wherever in this agreement Purchaser is appointed Owner's attorney-in-fact, such appointment is irrevocable.

14. Owner may not assign this agreement or any Source Contract or Derivative Contract, or any portion

thereof, except that if Owner should elect to assign or encumber the remaining balance of Owner's share of Proceeds, then in any transactions with third parties (a) this present agreement between Owner and Purchaser shall have precedence and any other arrangements shall be subject to this one, and (b) Purchaser shall have a right of first refusal to meet the substantial business terms of any third party offer for such remaining balance, as follows: Owner will furnish all necessary data and notify Purchaser in writing of any and each such third party offer (whether or not Purchaser has declined previous offers) and afford Purchaser thirty (30) days within which to make a substantially equal offer if Purchaser so elects and signifies in writing to Owner within the stated time period, accepting Purchaser's offer if it be forthcoming.

15. Purchaser shall have a right of first refusal, upon timing and with notification as set forth in paragraph 14(b) above, at any time to acquire the same or any lesser percentage of Owner's Proceeds from Source Contracts and Derivative Contracts, or to acquire any license(s) of production rights in the Property, in both cases with reference to the next two bona fide literary or other compositions created, shared, held or controlled by Owner in any medium anywhere and not otherwise governed by this agreement as Derivative Contracts, with the understanding that Purchaser's refusal to exercise such right in respect of the first composition shall not debar Purchaser from exercising it in respect of the second. Nothing in this agreement obligates Purchaser to exercise any right of first refusal or any other right or option granted Purchaser hereunder, or to effect production or exploitation or to seek enlargement of Proceeds in any way.

16. Purchaser undertakes no obligation or responsibility whatsoever for any costs, expenses, claims, legal compliances or other obligations arising in connection with the Property or its productions and other uses under any Source Contract(s) or Derivative

Contract(s), and Owner will indemnify and hold Purchaser harmless in respect of all such obligations. Nothing in this agreement is designed to constitute the parties joint venturers, partners or agents one to the other, or to create any taxable entity or right to pledge the other's credit.

17. Without affecting Purchaser's continuing and future share of Proceeds and other rights, the security assignment provided for in paragraph 12 above will terminate and the Property rights therein referred to will revert to Owner if and when Purchaser has actually received pursuant to this agreement an amount equal to one hundred and fifty percent (150%) of Purchaser's original payment made pursuant to paragraph 2 hereof. In those circumstances, and at Purchaser's option, Owner will assign and convey to Purchaser, to the extent permitted by then applicable laws, a share of Owner's copyright and other incorporeal rights in the Property parallel to and reflecting the percentage of Owner's share of Proceeds, or if such rights are not divisible in this way, an undivided share as joint Owner.

18. In connection with paragraph 17 above and equally with reference to payment of Purchaser's share of Proceeds, Purchaser will not bear any loss or diminution in value resulting from any change in the relative values of disparate currencies or exchange control regulations or local taxes anywhere between the date of this agreement and the date on which any of Purchaser's rights to receive Proceeds or other rights become vested.

19. Owner warrants and represents:

(a) That Owner is free lawfully to make this agreement without encumbrance or conflict of any nature, having acquired the rights hereinabove granted as follows:

(b) That the Property is original, unencumbered, free of infringing, libelous and other unlawful material and protected by copyright in the United States and elsewhere under the Universal Copyright and Berne Conventions;

(c) That Owner knows of no litigation, tax lien, adverse claim, clearance requirement, prospect of reversion or rights impediment or payment due a third party concerning the Property or any Source Contract or Derivative Contract;

(d) That the Exhibits annexed hereto constitute the entirety of relevant documentation to this transaction, that none of them has been altered, withdrawn, terminated, extended, encumbered, or in any way modified or affected directly or indirectly since their respective dates of coming into effect, and that each of them is an accurate copy of its original in the English language;

(e) That no conflicting grants exist or will be agreed or permitted by Owner;

(f) That all the rights assigned to Purchaser herein are lawfully assignable;

(g) That all rights granted to Purchaser herein are exclusive;

(h) That Owner knows of no impending substantial diminution in Proceeds measured against the two most recent Accountings, or of existing or impending lapses or flaws in legal protection of copyright or other rights in the Property anywhere.

Owner agrees (notwithstanding Purchaser's examination of the Exhibits) to indemnify and hold harmless Purchaser, Purchaser's directors, officers, agents, employees, associates, assignees and licensees against from and with respect to any and all claims, losses, damages, expenses (including reasonable counsel fees) and other liabilities arising out of or in connection with Owner's breach of any of the foregoing warranties or Purchaser's exercise of any rights granted to Purchaser hereunder, and any and all uses of the Property.

20. This Agreement, which with the Exhibits annexed fully sets forth the understanding between the

parties, is governed by the laws of _____ and may
not be altered except in writing, signed by each of the
parties hereto.

_____

(Owner)

Witness:

_____

_____

(Purchaser)

Comments

This form is designed for investment in established writings.
Buying shares of ongoing income streams together with specu-
lating in new works may attract those who prefer the banker's
approach as against the romance of production. A balanced
portfolio may engender better than average returns although
finding the winners is hard going.

Here the main points are:

1) Once again the transaction is set up under option.

2) The definitions aim at a variety of targets ranging from
contracts for the creation of income flow to the proceeds themselves.

3) Several of the clauses will almost surely be objectionable
and require modification, e.g. the right to make derivative works
in the Option Agreement and the requirement to sue infringers
in Paragraph 3c of the Purchase Agreement.

4) To the same effect, provisions such as Paragraph 9 may be
excusable only on grounds that there is no harm trying.

5) Paragraph 12 borrows from the film industry.

6) Paragraph 15 harpoons future works, but the investor
wants protection to balance its high risk.

Speculators in rights need a final reminder that choice of law is a key point. What California permits may be prohibited in much of Europe. Compulsory licenses may alter the position in a particular locale. EC and local British interpretations may take years being reconciled, and new laws in Asia may obstruct, suddenly, the relatively free spirit of American contract procedures. Nevertheless disharmony in global markets is no reason to stay home. Actually that would be impossible; communications were made for travel, and for leaping frontiers.

That being so, one makes special efforts with choice of law so as to appoint the right custodians.

We divide incorporeal empires into spheres, and appoint local governors for their administration. The world undergoes a new industrial revolution. There are still smokestacks, but over them invisible signals rush, distributing new forms of property.

Form G:
Contributions by
Licensees

FORM G: CONTRIBUTIONS BY LICENSEES

"DAI TOA SENDEN, K.K.

Date _____

Ridgefield Inc.
120 Spring Valley Road
Ridgefield, Conn., U.S.A.

Dear Sirs:
    The following fully sets forth our agreement, which is governed by the laws of New York, and may not be altered orally, concerning our "HOMBU"™ characters and their format, plots, dialogue, graphic representations, music, collective and individual names, locales and other forms and devices including without limitation the text published in book form by [name of publisher], all of which are hereinafter collectively referred to as "the Property" with the understanding that as between us we own outright all existing and future rights therein, throughout the world, of production, manufacture, recordation and reproduction by any act or method, copyright, trademark and patent whether such product consists of literary, dramatic,

musical, artistic, visual, mechanical or any other form of words, themes, ideas, compositions, creations, materials or products.

1. We warrant and represent that the Property is original, free of infringing, libelous and otherwise unlawful matter, and unencumbered in respect of television rights everywhere in the world.

You warrant and represent that you are free lawfully to make this agreement, and that all script, animation design and other material furnished by you as hereinafter set forth will be original except insofar as founded on the Property, unencumbered and free of infringing, libelous and other unlawful matter.

Each of us agrees to indemnify and hold harmless the other, its directors, officers, agents, associates, permitted assignees and permitted licensees against, from and in respect of any and all claims, losses, damages, expenses (including reasonable counsel fees) and other liabilities arising out of or in connection with its breach of any of its respective warranties or representations. Each of us may appear at any proceeding, action, or settlement negotiations for which idemnity might be sought pursuant to this paragraph 1, at no cost to the other, by counsel of its own choosing, and neither will settle any claim at the other's expense without the other's written consent.

2. In consideration of the limited license herein granted you to make television use of the Property, you agree to accomplish either of (a) or (b) below within the applicable time limit specified for its accomplishment, and to keep us reasonably advised of your progress: (a) no later than _____ , 19 ___ , and at no cost to us, to effect U.S. television network broadcast of no fewer than two (2) separately presented HOMBU episodes whether or not as part of an established on-going series, as prerecorded animated segments based on the Property in separate programs and in a form and in accordance with third-party arrangements all subject to our advance written approval which we may arbitrarily withhold; or (b) no later than _____ ,

19 ___, and at no cost to us, to complete production and delivery to us of a 24-minute storyboard including graphics and script based on segments of the Property and in form both subject to our advance written approval not to be unreasonably withheld. All material in (a) and (b) will bear appropriate copyright and trademark notices to be specified by us.

Your failure or refusal timely to meet the requirements of whichever alternative course you select between (a) and (b) above, subject in the case of (b) to reasonable delay caused by an event of *force majeure,* shall result automatically in termination of this agreement with expiration of all licenses hereunder and reversion of all rights to us, free of obligation and encumbrance, together with valid assignment outright and prepaid delivery to us (which you hereby appoint us to effect in your name as attorney-in-fact in the event of your failure or refusal) of all storyboards, sketches and other physical elements relating to the Property theretofore created by you or with your authorization, and valid assignment outright to us (with similar authorization to act in your name and stead) of copyright and all other rights in and to Ridgefield Material as defined in paragraph 8 hereof, but free of any obligation to pay you for its use in any medium anywhere. In the event no significant physical or incorporeal material has been created and thus made available to us following your default in timely accomplishment of your choice between (a) and (b) then your sole liability shall be payment to us of One Thousand ($1,000) Dollars, reflecting in our mutual view the fair market value of an option covering the time period specified in (b) above.

Paragraphs 3 through 14, inclusive, of this agreement deal with what consequences ensue provided and on the assumption that you shall in fact have fulfilled your obligations as agreed to under (a) or (b) above.

3. Subject to the provisions of the subparagraph immediately preceding this paragraph 3, we hereby grant to you the exclusive option, to be exercised, if you so elect, by furnishing us with written notice to

that effect by the close of regular business hours no later than one hundred fifty (150) days following your complete accomplishment of obligations under paragraph 2(a) or (b), to produce either the special(s) provided for in paragraph 6 hereof or an animated color series of at least thirteen (13) videotape or film television programs based on the Property and each of not less than twenty-four (24) minutes running time exclusive of commerical matter, upon the following terms and conditions:

(a) Notice of option exercise, to be effective, must be accompanied by payment in the amount of Five Thousand ($5,000) Dollars constituting a non-returnable advance against royalties specified below;

(b) The series format, title, music, graphic designs, fictional characters, successive story outlines, episode by episode, and billing credit together with your financing and distribution arrangements with third parties all will be subject on a continuing basis to our advance written approval, which shall not be unreasonably withheld;

(c) As between us you shall own the physical recordings of the series programs with the exclusive right, subject to paragraph 3(b) above, to arrange their distribution throughout the world perpetually in all existing and future media except that you may not without our advance written consent, which we may arbitrarily withhold, authorize use of such recordings anywhere outside the United States, its territories, possessions and Commonwealths and Canada (hereinafter collectively referred to as "the territory"), or authorize their use in any medium except "free" network television or syndicated television (i.e., reaching at least six major markets) within the recited territory, reflecting our mutual intent to impound, subject to future negotiation, uses in other territories and media;

(d) Your rights to use the Property shall automatically expire, making your ownership of the physical program recordings sterile, unless initial television broadcast of the first series program within the recited confines shall have occurred within three hundred sixty five (365) days from the effective exercise of your option as part of a firm third-party order, whose requirement of additional options, however, we will accept, provided approvals and the other conditions of this agreement be preserved and provided further that annually compounded royalty increases, pursuant to then current industry practice, accompany the option structure, which in turn may not permit any series reorders whatever for a total of more than five (5) years or any broadcasting hiatus of more than thirteen (13) weeks;

(e) You will arrange that each program episode in the series visually display copyright notice and that contracts with licensees will require such copyright notice sufficient for protection under § 17 U.S.C. § 101, *et seq.* and the Universal Copyright Convention, together with lawful trademark and other legends in our name or in the name(s) of our designees as we advise you in writing from time to time in concert with your production and editing schedules insofar as we are kept aware of them;

(f) (i) For each run of any program episode in the series within the specified territory, and allowing first for the recovery of the advance paid us pursuant to paragraph 3(a) above, we shall receive within ten (10) days following the date scheduled for initial telecast of the applicable program episode a royalty in the sum of Two Thousand Five Hundred ($2,500) Dollars for a half-hour program or a royalty of Ten Thousand ($10,000) Dollars for a half-hour special, with residuals in each case payable within ten (10) days of initial broadcast commencing the next successive run, if any, based on the following percentages of initial compensation for that program episode: second run, no residual royalty; third run, fifty (50%) percent; fourth run and all succeeding runs, twenty-five (25%) percent. Payment for a run encompasses payment for television broadcast once over every station within the recited territory;

(ii) As additional compensation beyond royalties payable to us in connection with any series or special hereunder, and with both, we shall be entitled to receive as and when received by you in U.S. dollars, with our share of any blocked funds abroad held in trust for our account, sums equal to forty (40%) percent of your share of net profits but in no event less than twenty (20%) percent of one hundred (100%) percent thereof derived from each such series and special, net profits to be defined as defined in your agreement with your network or other financier-distributor but allowing in any event for deductions, before net profits are arrived at, of all production costs, royalties, distribution fees, profit shares payable to others and other elements excluding overhead which are customarily deducted before net profits are determined. We shall be entitled to copies of relevant accountings furnished you by your distributors and to inspect, at reasonable business hours, those portions of your books and records that relate to transactions arising from such use of the Property. Our share of net profits will be increased to fifty (50%) percent if we or any of our principals shall effectively introduce major sponsorship or production financing in connection with the contemplated special(s) or series, whichever is applicable;

(g) At our request you will afford our principals an opportunity to write or collaborate in the writing of mutually agreed program episodes for additional compensation and credit at least equal to the applicable minima prescribed by the then current Basic Agreement of the Writers Guild, and you will, wherever feasible, use music and lyrics furnished by us or by our designee in connection with the programs;

(h) While our relationship under the license agreement is not designed to create any joint venture, partnership, agency or taxable entity or to burden us with any of your production costs, liabilities or responsibilities of union compliances, you agree at our request to negotiate co-production arrangements with us and to that end will not locate the production situs outside the New York-Connecticut area without our advance reasonable approval which approval shall not be unreasonably withheld.

4. We have advised you that we have exposed the Property in book form to _____ Television Network and you have advised us that _____ has a 14-day right of first refusal concerning your television programs. With that background, you agree that if you elect and pursue the course provided for in paragraph 2(a) above, and if, before you have effectively exercised your option pursuant to paragraph 3 above, a network or other licensee makes us a firm series offer requiring the use of Ridgefield Material as hereinafter defined, but rejecting your company as the production entity, then you agree to negotiate with us and/or with the offeror concerning your services as animation supervisor for the series, but in any event, and without committing yourself to render further service, you agree that we may on a continuing basis use theretofore created Ridgefield Material and all its component elements in the series subject to paying you twenty (20%) percent of the royalties received by us for licensing the Property in that form, for as long as Ridgefield Material is used in the series, and with a right on your part to be furnished with copies of series royalty statements received by us and to inspect, at reasonable business hours, those portions of our books and records that relate to the series royalties.

5. We may nevertheless at any time before your effective option exercise accept a rival offer for an animated television series which severs the Proprty from Ridgefield Material and contemplates different animation and writing, by paying you your verified costs incurred in connection with compliance with paragraph 2(a) or (b) above, plus three (3%) percent of our share of future net receipts from television and merchandising sources received by us in U.S. dollars from exploitation of the Property in those media, for your services to that date, thereby terminating this agreement and leaving each of us with no further obligation to the other. Our preemptive right under this paragraph 5 shall dissolve upon your effective exercise of the option in paragraph 3.

6. Notwithstanding anything to the contrary set forth in this agreement, but subject to the same approvals, territorial and media restrictions, copyright provisions and other restrictions, and to fulfillment of the conditions in paragraph 2(a) or (b) above, you may alternatively exercise the option granted you in paragraph 3 above so as to acquire the rights to produce no fewer than two (2) specials based on the Property each of which shall be not less than twenty-four (24) minutes duration for U.S. television only. In those circumstances your notice of option exercise must specify your election to produce specials and be accompanied by a nonreturnable advance payment of Five Thousand ($5,000) Dollars against royalties of Ten Thousand ($10,000) Dollars for each special, the balance of Five Thousand ($5,000) Dollars payable on the commencement of production, with residual payments corresponding to the percentages earlier set forth in connection with series episodes but based on original compensation for each special. The last authorized special must, to avoid reversion of our rights, be televised as specified no later than three hundred sixty-five (365) days following your exercise of the single option for multiple specials and in any event we must be fully compensated for all the specials by payment to us of the full balance remaining, less advances theretofore received, no later than forty-five (45) days following your furnishing of notice. Provided you shall have fulfilled these conditions, your series option shall revive and be available to you on the earlier specified terms and conditions including without limitation, the furnishing of written notice and payment of the advance specified in paragraph 3(a) above, for a period of one hundred fifty (150) days following our receipt of the entire minimum guaranteed payment for the special(s). Our total initial compensation for successive specials shall rise by five (5%) percent compounded with each special, advance payments rising commensurately, and our share of net profits as earlier provided shall also be payable in respect of each special.

7. We reserve all rights not explicitly granted to you in this agreement including without limitation all

copyrights, trademarks, fictional character and name rights and the exclusive rights to dispose of the Property at any time anywhere without restriction and without compensation to you (subject to paragraph 5 if applicable), unless we elect to use Ridgefield Material as set forth below. Our reserved rights include without limitation the media of merchandising, feature films, music and book publication, live performance and television other than in animated form. Your rights licensed under this agreement, however, are exclusive in respect of animated television subject to our preemptive rights pursuant to paragraph 5 above and to your compliance with the other provisions hereof, reverting to us automatically in any event upon the completion of television use authorized hereunder if not earlier terminated pursuant to other terms hereof such as your breach or non-exercise of any option available to you as provided.

8. Those original literary, visual, musical and other elements, including approved new characters, if any, which you engraft on the Property in connection with the program(s), and which meet the standards of "derivative work" as defined in 90 Stat. 2541, 17 U.S.C. § 101 are referred to in this Agreement as Ridgefield Material and shall belong to us and remain unavailable for your use without our written consent, except as "fixed" in your program recording in accordance with the above license grant, on the ground that we own the underlying material on which your adaptation is based. No mandatory merger between your derivative and our primary material occurs, except at our election from time to time so that we may at any time arrange and use animated and other derivative versions of our underlying material with and by others, without limiting our rights to use public domain material as well, and equally we may use your original derivative contributions to our underlying primary material even though your own use thereof is prohibited for the recited reasons. You agree that all Ridgefield Material, from the moment of its creation, shall be impressed with a trust in our favor and you agree promptly and continuously at our cost to assign the copyright and

all other rights in and to the Ridgefield Material to us for the full term of copyright and extensions thereof, by proper and effective instruments, hereby appointing us irrevocably your attorney-in-fact to do so in your name and stead in the event of your failure or refusal, to the end that we own and may, but need not, use Ridgefield Material fully or in part perpetually throughout the world in all existing and future media and in any form, language and frame of our sole choosing, without restriction but subject to compensating you for its use only in the circumstances explicitly recited in this agreement as requiring payment.

We shall not be obligated to pay you for the use of Ridgefield Material on any television program or series produced by you, or for its use in any medium anywhere if you fail to meet your obligations under paragraph 2(a) or (b), or if having met them you fail or decline timely to exercise your option available to you under paragraph 3, or if you are in substantial breach of this Agreement. We shall, however, be required to compensate you for the television use of Ridgefield Material under the conditions set forth in paragraph 4 and for certain merchandising uses as follows.

9. "Merchandising Revenues" are defined as licensing fees received by us or for our benefit from sources within the territory encompassed by this Agreement in U.S. dollars and arising from the licensing of merchandising tie-ups of the Property in connection with various products such as toys and clothing excluding, however, phonograms, books, cartoon strips, and other products of the print media, anywhere within the territory, and subject to deduction of the following elements before your share is arrived at: (a) fees and costs payable to distributors and agents; (b) all percentage shares and flat payments contractually payable to others, and (c) local taxes, import and export duties and shipping charges, including insurance.

Provided you shall have met your obligations under paragraph 2(a) or (b), and shall have made timely exercise of the option granted you pursuant to paragraph 3, and provided further, that all payments due us as the result of your exercise of such option have been made, and you are not in breach of any substantial provision of this Agreement, then you shall prospectively but not retroactively, as of the next accounting and with no allowance for recoupment of any advance previously paid us by merchandising organizations, become entitled to share in Merchandising Revenues arising from licensing of the Property and substantially as distinguished from incidentally utilizing Ridgefield Material as follows, with rights to copies of accountings and rights of inspection similar to those earlier provided:

Amount	Your Percentage
First $50,000	5
Second $50,000	10
Third $50,000	15
Fourth $50,000	17
Fifth $50,000	19
Sixth and all further units of $50,000 (i.e., from $250,000 upwards)	20

If the aggregate of the Merchandising Revenues in which you are entitled to share reaches Three Hundred Thousand ($300,000) Dollars:

(a) Your percentage of such Merchandising Revenues thereafter shall remain at twenty (20%) percent for the three-year period commencing with the first calendar year following the year in which the Three Hundred Thousand ($300,000) Dollar amount is reached;

(b) With respect to each year after the end of that three-year period your percentage of such Merchandising Revenues shall be ten (10%) percent.

Nothing in the foregoing constitutes any implied assurance that such Merchandising Revenues will reach sufficient volume to become divisible, and any shares thereof contracted as payable to production elements will be borne out of your share.

If you shall have effectively exercised your option pursuant to paragraph 3 above, having met its preconditions and making the required advance payment simultaneously with its exercise, and if one or more programs based on the Property and produced by you shall in fact have been telecast either on a U.S. national network or at least once each in six major markets, then you shall become prospectively but not retroactively entitled as provided in this paragraph 9 to share in Merchandising Revenues from our licensing of the Property which as the result of our invocation of rights under paragraph 8 to discard your contributions does not substantially use Ridgefield Material. In these circumstances your share of Merchandising Revenues as defined in paragraph 9 shall be three (3%) percent and you shall be entitled to copies of accountings and rights of inspection parallel to those available to you when Ridgefield Material is substantially utilized. Nothing in this paragraph or elsewhere in this Agreement entitles you to share Merchandising Revenues from licenses entered into before your qualification to share Merchandising Revenues as the result of meeting the specified conditions.

10. In all of the concomitant circumstances vesting in you a right to share Merchandising Revenues as provided in paragraph 9 above, and subject to any television series agreement with a network or other third party arrived at as provided elsewhere in this agreement, your series option available under paragraph 3 insofar as it relates only to a series shall revive and be available to you, under the same conditions including approvals and payments as earlier provided, in respect of any "spin-off" series, based on the Property and authorized by us to be presented in animated form with time limits for accomplishment of the various steps extended commensurately to parallel those provided for concerning your original series option, and with the understanding that your spin-off option granted pursuant to this paragraph terminates in any event if not effectively exercised no later than six (6) months from initial U.S. television network

broadcast or initial U.S. television syndicated run of the last series cycle or special available for production by you as provided elsewhere in this agreement, or from the vesting of your option to produce a spin-off series based on the Property, whichever is sooner. Ridgefield Material in any spin-off series will vest in us and be governed by all of the same provisions that govern Ridgefield Material created in connection with other programming hereunder.

11. Either of us and both may assign this agreement fully or in part to an entity in which our respective principals have a controlling interest, remaining liable, however, for performance of any unfulfilled obligations if the assignee defaults.

12. Each of us may use the other's name and the names, likenesses and professional data concerning the other's principals to announce the association created by this agreement and otherwise in furtherance of its terms, but not as an endorsement of any product or service.

13. Whether and in what degree you shall have become entitled to share in Merchandising Revenues pursuant to paragraph 9, including determination whether Ridgefield Material is substantially, as distinguished from incidentally, utilized as specified therein, shall in the event of dispute be submitted to arbitration by a single arbitrator in New York City under the rules then obtaining of the American Arbitration Association and a mutually agreed upon law firm shall have the right to hold the disputed monies until the resolution of such dispute. The arbitrator shall be selected within two (2) business days after such submission and the arbitration hearing shall be held within three (3) business days after the filing of the demand for arbitration. The arbitrator shall be instructed to proceed and to render an award forthwith. Any award of the arbitrator in favor of Ridgefield under this paragraph 13 shall be limited to an award of compensation not to exceed that provided in this

Agreement. The decision of the arbitrator shall be final and binding and judgment on the award rendered may be entered in any court having jurisdiction.

14. Unless written change of address notification is furnished, any written notices one to the other hereunder are to be addressed:

(a) To you, at the address heading on this letter;

(b) To us, c/o _____ or in each case to the changed address specified in writing.

Very truly yours
DAI TOA SENDEN, K.K.

By _____

AGREED TO:
RIDGEFIELD, INC.

By _____

Comments

We have here a transaction where licensee accomplishments are acknowledged, but with elaborate caution. First Toa, the Japanese owner of "Hombu" characters, commissions an American animation packager for the addition of new material we may call "Implant" generally and "Engraft" if the material is severable, "Influx" if the attachment is made permanent by contract. Commercial possibilities are nearly endless. The first television series may be re-created in different countries under format license. New characters may be introduced. One element may unexpectedly succeed in local merchandising. Anything may happen, and somewhere along the line it may turn out that a local contributor supplies the magic touch. In those circumstances we need contract machinery in place. Familiar concepts appear in the form presented. More specifically, these points may be noted:

1) The contract explicitly hinges the licensee's position on actual use of its material, which is subject to severance (clause 5, and the phrase "unless we elect to use" in 7).

2) The Japanese owner not only reserves ownership of its underlying material but impresses new variants with equitable trusts in terms that may seem foreign to European lawyers.

3) Paragraphs 4, 5 and 9 provide what amounts to alimony if the owner severs.

4) What if Toa secured satellite rights to a championship chess match between a Russian and a computer? Straight television forms, everybody might think, but when it came down to the clearances it would be interesting to remember some German monographs contending for copyright in the actual chess games, more complex here with a computer as joint author. Somewhere in Toa's distribution sphere, if not in Japan, concepts of this sort may have become law.

Form H:
A Corporate
Warranty

FORM H: A CORPORATE WARRANTY

COPYRIGHTS, PATENTS, TRADEMARKS AND SERVICE MARKS

Schedule X is a complete list of all copyrights, patents, trademarks, service marks and trade names, and all registrations issued, and applications for registration pending, with respect to any of the foregoing, throughout the world (collectively "Rights"), that relate to or are used in or are proposed for use in connection with the conduct of the business of the Company throughout the world, all of which Rights the Company owns or is using and has the right to use under valid licenses, as indicated in Schedule X. The expiration and renewal dates, if any, of the Rights are set forth in Schedule X. None of the Rights is subject to any pending or, to the knowledge of the Company, threatened challenge or reversion, and the consummation of the transactions contemplated by this Agreement will not result in any change in the terms or provisions thereof or create any right of termination, cancellation or reversion with respect thereto anywhere in the world. The Rights do not infringe or conflict with the rights of any other person and the Company is not

aware of any infringement or violation of any right of
the Company by any other person with respect to the
Rights. Except as set forth in Schedule X, no person
or entity other than the Company has any right to use,
license, sublicense or operate under any of the Rights.
The Company has exercised quality control with
respect to all Rights licensed by the Company to the
extent necessary to preserve the validity of such
Rights. The Company has heretofore provided to the
Buyer complete and correct copies of each license
agreement relating to the Rights.

Schedule Y hereto contains a true and complete
list of (i) each literary work, including, without
limitation, tapes and other recordings, currently published by, or under the authorization of, the Company,
including, without limitation, periodic and irregular
serial publications, special editions, limited editions,
regional editions and foreign editions, together with
the frequency of issue and ISSN Number of each such
Publication, and (ii) all contemplated future publications of the Company, together with a brief description
of their subject matter and format and the titles
currently assigned to them, currently planned or under
consideration by the Company (collectively, the "Publications"). The Company is and will be the sole,
absolute and exclusive owner, free of any lien,
encumbrance, claim, equity or contractual commitment, except as disclosed in Schedule Y of all rights
to publish, produce, sell, license, adapt for other
media, alter, create composites or anthologies from
and otherwise utilize the Publications and all of their
component elements (except advertising material appearing therein) including, without limitation, text,
titles, informational data, photographs and graphic
depictions, in any and all existing and future forms,
languages and media throughout the world, including,
without limitation, free, pay and cable television, video
cassette, compact- or video-disc, feature films, live
performance and merchandising tie-ups, together with
all databases held by or used in the Publishing
Business. All issues of the Publications existing on the
date hereof have been, and all issues of the

Publications existing on the Closing Date will have been, imprinted with such notices as conform to and afford maximum protection under the copyright laws of the United States of America and the Universal Copyright Convention, and the Company is and will be the sole, absolute and exclusive owner of the copyright therein. The Company is and will be the sole, absolute and exclusive owner of the titles of the Publications, and all trademarks, service marks, logos, devices, insignias and formats associated with the Publications, and the goodwill relating thereto, and, except as disclosed in Schedule Y has not granted any right, title or interest therein to any person. Schedule Y contains a correct and complete list of all registrations and pending applications for the trademarks, service marks, logos, devices, insignias and formats described in the preceding sentence. All material except advertising material, including, without limitation, text, photographs and graphics, which appears in copies of the Publications existing on the date thereof, in process or commissioned or contracted for with respect to future issues of the Publications, or held in the files of the Company, were created as works for hire or have been assigned to the Company outright without reservation of rights, and are and will be the sole, absolute and exclusive property of the Company, and the Company has no obligation to pay any royalty, license fee, commission or other amount, howsoever characterized, or to obtain any third-party clearances or consents in respect of any past or future use of such material except as set forth in Schedule Y. All persons whose names or likenesses appear in existing issues of the Publications or which are held by the Company for possible use in future issues of the Publications have executed and delivered valid and sufficient full releases of their rights in such names or likenesses to the extent such releases are necessary. Except as set forth in Schedule Y there are no agreements relating to the Publications to which the Company is a party or by which it is bound, including, without limitation, any agreements for the provision of paper, printing, photoengraving, color separation, binding, circulation

fulfillment or single copy distribution of the Publications, or with authors, correspondents, reviewers, editors, contributors, photographers, illustrators or holders
of subsidiary or derivative rights. Complete and correct
copies of all agreements listed in Schedule Y have
heretofore been delivered to the Buyer. Schedule Y also
sets forth a complete and correct schedule of all
unearned advances outstanding as at _____
paid to authors, correspondents, reviewers, editors,
contributors, photographers and illustrators listed on
Schedule Y.

Comments

This form is rather different from the others, being one
provision rather than the entirety of an agreement, and reflecting the world of corporate mergers and acquisitions which it
inhabits. Any takeover requires special care. There is no such
thing as overly great suspicion, and as a consequence, the warranty provisions stand large out of proportion as monuments to
mistrust. All too often the contracts unearthed by the acquiring
company turn out like what appears under garden rocks when
these are rolled away, a colony of lower forms better left unseen,
but the corporate acquisition goes forward anyway, at least with
purchase of assets if not of shares, and the lawyers load up on
warranties to make up for the contracts missing from the portfolio they have been instructed to acquire. Presumably one has
no knowledge that any warranties are actually untrue.

The foregoing sample from a publishing takeover is nearly
self-explanatory. Exhibits are omitted, and several points need
to be mentioned:

1) Schedules X and Y, together with clauses introducing
them, will need scrutiny to escape what may well be duplication
if not outright inconsistency.

2) With these difficulties sorted out, we recognize companions from earlier text, assurances concerning everything from
rights to residuals.

3) Presumably "adapt . . . alter, create composites" takes care of the *droit moral* but explicit waiver of this element in a different clause would afford further comfort.

4) It may turn out profitable to consider what the quoted warranties leave untouched, the possibility that under one national system or another the Berne Convention, or its local implements, may permit waivers and other advantages which the company being acquired could warrant as having been effectively secured from its authors. This is relatively new territory. Most acquirees will of course have secured nothing close to the desired protections, but there can be no harm trying.

INDEX

189